American Literature in Context
from 1865 to 1929

Literature in Context

Literature in Context is an important new series that provides readers with relevant historical knowledge that deepens their understanding of American and British literature. Each accessible volume discusses the issues and events that engaged writers and provides original and useful readings of important literary works that demonstrate how context contributes to meaning.

American Literature in Context
from 1865 to 1929

Philip R. Yannella

WILEY-BLACKWELL

A John Wiley & Sons, Ltd., Publication

Blackwell Publishing was acquired by John Wiley & Sons in February 2007. Blackwell's
publishing program has been merged with Wiley's global Scientific, Technical, and Medical
business to form Wiley-Blackwell.

Registered Office
John Wiley & Sons Ltd, The Atrium, Southern Gate, Chichester, West Sussex, PO19 8SQ,
United Kingdom

Editorial Offices
350 Main Street, Malden, MA 02148-5020, USA

9600 Garsington Road, Oxford, OX4 2DQ, UK

The Atrium, Southern Gate, Chichester, West Sussex, PO19 8SQ, UK

For details of our global editorial offices, for customer services, and for information about how
to apply for permission to reuse the copyright material in this book please see our website at
www.wiley.com/wiley-blackwell.

The right of Philip R. Yannella to be identified as the author of this work has been asserted in
accordance with the UK Copyright, Designs and Patents Act 1988.

Wiley also publishes its books in a variety of electronic formats. Some content that appears in
print may not be available in electronic books.

Designations used by companies to distinguish their products are often claimed as trademarks.
All brand names and product names used in this book are trade names, service marks,
trademarks or registered trademarks of their respective owners. The publisher is not associated
with any product or vendor mentioned in this book. This publication is designed to provide
accurate and authoritative information in regard to the subject matter covered. It is sold on
the understanding that the publisher is not engaged in rendering professional services. If
professional advice or other expert assistance is required, the services of a competent
professional should be sought.

Library of Congress Cataloging-in-Publication Data

Yannella, Philip.
  American literature in context from 1865 to 1929 / Philip R. Yannella.
      p. cm. – (Literature in context)
  Includes bibliographical references and index.
  ISBN 978-1-4051-6781-9 (alk. paper) – ISBN 978-1-4051-6780-2 (pbk. : alk.
paper) 1. American literature–19th century–History and criticism.   2. American literature–
20th century–History and criticism.   3. National characteristics, American, in literature.
4. Literature and history–United States.   5. American literature.   I. Title.
  PS214.Y36 2010
  810.9'358738–dc22

                                                                              2010003199

A catalogue record for this book is available from the British Library.

Set in 10.5 on 13pt Minion by Toppan Best-set Premedia Limited
Printed and bound in Malaysia by Vivar Printing Sdn Bhd

1   2011

For

Sook Kyung Kim

Contents

Timeline of Texts and Historical Events

Texts	Historical Events
1865. Walt Whitman, "When Lilacs Last in the Dooryard Bloomed"	**1865.** Civil War ends with surrender of Confederate General Robert E. Lee to Union forces on April 9. President Lincoln shot on April 14 and dies the next day. Reconstruction of the South begins.
1866. Walt Whitman, *Drum Taps*	**1866.** First riots (also known as "massacres") against extension of civil rights to blacks take place in Norfolk, Virginia, Memphis, Tennessee, and New Orleans, Louisiana.
1868. Louisa May Alcott, *Little Women*	Ku Klux Klan founded. 1,200 Irish-Catholic veterans of Civil War, formed into American wing of the Irish Revolutionary Brotherhood, march into Canada to strike a blow against Great Britain and are quickly defeated.
	1871. 12,000 buildings burned in Chicago fire.
1872. Walt Whitman, *Democratic Vistas* Mark Twain, *Roughing It*	"Orange Riot" in New York pits Irish Catholics against Irish Protestants; more riots involving Irish Catholics occur in subsequent years.

Texts	Historical Events
1873. Mark Twain and Charles Dudley Warner, *The Gilded Age*	**1873.** Major depression begins. **1873–76.** Large antiblack riots in Mississippi, Louisiana, and South Carolina. **1874.** Founding of the Women's Christian Temperance Union.
1875. Charles Nordhoff, *The Communistic Societies of the United States*	**1876.** Centennial Exposition held in Philadelphia. General George A. Custer and his troops defeated at the Battle of the Little Bighorn by a combined Lakota-Northern Cheyenne force. Reconstruction ends after the presidential election. **1877.** Strikes halt railroads across much of the US.
1879. Henry George, *Progress and Poverty* Henry James, *Daisy Miller: A Study* **1881.** Walt Whitman, *Specimen Days* **1881–4.** Helen Hunt Jackson publishes work on the treatment of Native Americans: *A Century of Dishonor* (1881), *Report on the Conditions and Needs of the Mission Indians* (1883), *Ramona* (1884) **1885.** Mark Twain, *The Adventures of Huckleberry Finn*	**1882.** Chinese Exclusion Act passed. **1883.** Supreme Court of the US declares unconstitutional the Civil Rights Act of 1875, which had prohibited segregation. **1884-1887.** *Century Magazine* publishes extensive articles on Civil War, later collected as four-volume *Battles and Leaders of the Civil War.*
1886. Sara Orne Jewett, "A White Heron" **1887.** Edward Bellamy, *Looking Backward* Charles W. Chesnutt, "The Goophered Grapevine"	**1886.** Haymarket "affair." American Federation of Labor is founded.

Texts	Historical Events
1889. Ambrose Bierce's "Chickamauga" Charles W. Chesnutt, *The Conjure Woman* and "What is a White Man?" Andrew Carnegie, "Wealth"	**1889.** In September, Civil War Battle of Chickamauga commemorated (one of many commemorative events stressing the reconciliation of North and South).
1890. Jacob Riis, *How the Other Half Lives*	**1890.** 22 cities have more than 100,000 residents. US Census Bureau defines an "urban" place as a city or other incorporated place having 2,500 or more residents. It will continue to define "urban" that way in subsequent censuses.
1891. Hamlin Garland, *Main-Travelled Roads* Pope Leo XIII, *De Rerum Novarum* ("Of New Things") Mary E. Wilkins Freeman, "The Revolt of 'Mother'" and "A New England Nun"	**1891.** Mass lynching of 11 Italian immigrants in New Orleans.
1892. Ambrose Bierce, *Tales of Soldiers and Civilians* Charlotte Perkins Gilman, "The Yellow Wall Paper"	**1892.** Strike at Andrew Carnegie's Homestead Steel Works in western Pennsylvania.
1893. Finley Peter Dunne, first Mr. Dooley column Stephen Crane, *Maggie: A Girl of the Streets*	**1893.** Chicago World's Fair. Major depression begins. Industrial "armies" of the unemployed are formed in western states. Strike against Pullman Palace Car Company expands to close the US railroad system.
1894. William Dean Howells, *A Traveler from Altruria* **1895.** Booker T. Washington, "Atlanta Compromise" Stephen Crane, *The Red Badge of Courage*	

Texts	Historical Events
1896. Abraham Cahan, *Yekl: A Tale of the New York Ghetto* **1897.** Sara Orne Jewett, "Martha's Lady" Harold Frederic, *The Damnation of Theron Ware* Charlotte Perkins Gilman, *Women and Economics* Edward Bellamy, *Equality* **1898.** Abraham Cahan, *The Imported Bridegroom and Other Stories* **1899.** W. E. B. DuBois, *The Philadelphia Negro: A Social Study* Edwin Markham, "The Man with the Hoe" Thorstein Veblen, *The Theory of the Leisure Class* Frank Norris, *McTeague* Edith Wharton, "Souls Belated" Kate Chopin, *The Awakening* **1900.** Theodore Dreiser, *Sister Carrie* **1901.** Mark Twain, "The United States of Lyncherdom" Charles W. Chesnutt, *The Marrow of Tradition* W. E. B. DuBois publishes a series of four articles in the *New York Times Magazine* on the situation of blacks in New York, Philadelphia, and Boston	**1896.** In *Plessy v. Ferguson*, Supreme Court of the US finds that separate but equal facilities for blacks and whites are Constitutional. "Populism," as represented by the People's Party, is at its height. **1898.** Spanish–American War **1899.** Supreme Court extends its "separate but equal" doctrine to educational facilities. **1899–1922.** 3,436 people lynched in the US; anti-black riots occur with great frequency in both the South and the North. **1901.** President William McKinley assassinated by anarchist Leon Czolgosz. Founding of the Socialist Party of America.

Texts	Historical Events
1903. Lillian Pettingill, *Toilers of the Home: The Record of a College Woman's Experience as a Domestic Servant* W. E. B. DuBois, *The Souls of Black Folk* and "The Talented Tenth"	**1903.** A year of heightened labor-management conflict – during that year, there were 3,648 strikes involving 788,000 workers (8.4 percent of the workforce).
1904. Lincoln Steffens, *The Shame of the Cities*	
1905. Thomas F. Dixon, Jr., *The Clansman*	**1905.** Industrial Workers of the World founded.
1906. Upton Sinclair, *The Jungle*	**1906.** San Francisco earthquake and subsequent fire.
1907. Henry James, *The American Scene*	**1907.** Peak year for immigration. Press reports that New York now has the largest concentration of Jewish people in the world.
1909. Gertrude Stein, *Three Lives* Jack London, "South of the Slot"	
	1910. Press reports that about 400,000 immigrants return to their home countries each year. According to the Census Bureau, 26% of US residents live in the 100 largest cities, up from 21% in 1890
1911. Edith Wharton, *Ethan Frome*	
1912. Theodore Dreiser, *The Financier* Mary Antin, *The Promised Land*	**1912.** Lawrence, Massachusetts textile factories strike.
1913. Willa Cather, *O Pioneers!* Jack London, *John Barleycorn* Robert Frost, *A Boy's Will*	**1913.** Paterson, NJ silk mills strike. State-wide strike in Colorado against Colorado Fuel and Iron Company. For the 12th time since 1894, martial law is declared in Colorado.
1914. Theodore Dreiser, *The Titan* Robert Frost, *North of Boston*	**1914.** World War I (i.e., the Great War) begins in August.

Texts	Historical Events
1915. Carl Sandburg, "That Walsh Report" Ralph Chaplin, "Solidarity Forever" Charlotte Perkins Gilman, *Herland*	**1915.** Commemoration of 50th anniversary of the end of the Civil War. *The Birth of a Nation* released in March. Leo M. Frank lynched outside Marietta, Georgia in August. Execution of Industrial Workers of the World songwriter/poet Joe Hill in Utah. Founding of new Ku Klux Klan in November. **1915–20.** "Strike fever" in the US. Year after year, there are increasing numbers of strikes.
1916. Carl Sandburg, *Chicago and Other Poems* Robert Frost, *Mountain Interval*	**1916.** Report of the United States Congressional Commission on Industrial Relations says that widespread "industrial unrest" is caused by high unemployment, a court system prejudiced against working people, the fact that workers are prevented from unionizing, and the inequitable distribution of wealth and income. **1917.** US enters World War I in April. Socialist Party of America pledges its opposition to the war. In June, Espionage Act is passed by government, criminalizing some forms of war opposition; government surveillance of war opponents begins. Bolshevik Revolution in Russia. Immigration Act of 1917 bars Asian immigration from a number of areas not affected by previous restrictions.

Texts	Historical Events
1918. Edith Wharton, *Summer* Willa Cather, *My Antonia*	**1918.** Influenza pandemic. World War I ends in November. Bolshevik leader Lenin writes "Letter to American Workingmen," telling them they should now join the international revolution of the working class.
1919. Sherwood Anderson, *Winesburg, Ohio* John Reed, *Ten Days That Shook the World* Anzia Yezierska, "The Fat of the Land"	**1919.** Raids by Department of Justice – the Palmer Raids – on radical offices in many cities. Record-breaking numbers of strikes. More than 4 million workers, about 20% of the workforce, are out on strike during 1919. Major race riots between May and October. Outcome of baseball World Series fixed by gamblers and some Chicago White Sox players. Wall Street bombing in September. Deportation of 240 alien anarchists in December.
1920. Edith Wharton, *The Age of Innocence* F. Scott Fitzgerald, "May Day" and *This Side of Paradise* Sinclair Lewis, *Main Street*	**1920.** Eighteenth Amendment to the US Constitution goes into effect, prohibiting the manufacture and distribution of alcohol. Nineteenth Amendment to the US Constitution is ratified, giving women full voting rights.
1922. Sinclair Lewis, *Babbitt* William Carlos Williams, *Spring and All* Katherine Anne Porter, "Maria Concepcion" Harold Stearns (ed.) *Civilization in the United States: An Inquiry by Thirty Americans*	**1921.** First Quota Act passed, fixing the annual number of people of particular national groups permitted entry to the US (in 1924 and 1929, similar legislation lowered the quotas).

Texts	Historical Events
1923. Upton Sinclair, *The Goose-Step: A Study of American Higher Education* Anzia Yezierska *Children of Loneliness* Jean Toomer, *Cane* **1925.** F. Scott Fitzgerald, *The Great Gatsby* Willa Cather, *The Professor's House* Anzia Yezierska *Bread Givers* Sherwood Anderson, *Dark Laughter* **1926.** Langston Hughes, *The Weary Blues* Ernest Hemingway, *The Sun Also Rises* and *The Torrents of Spring* **1929.** Nella Larsen, *Passing*	**1923.** Press reports indicate Ku Klux Klan has developed a great deal of electoral power in some states. **1926–9.** Press reports about widespread prosperity in the US. **1927.** Executions of Sacco and Vanzetti. **1929.** The Hoover Committee, chaired by President Hoover himself, publishes treatise titled *Recent Economic Changes in the United States*, which emphasizes the economic expansion but notes that its effect has been "spotty," that some US regions and industries continue to experience difficulties, and that farmers, whose families comprise some 30 percent of the population, have "suffered severely in the years since 1920." In his Memorial Day speech in Gettysburg, Pennsylvania, Secretary of Labor James J. Davis says that there are still many Americans who are "enslaved" as underpaid workers. Stock Market Crash and beginning of Great Depression.

Introduction

Much of the most significant American literature produced in the 1865–1929 period was engaged with the great social issues of the day. Some of this writing was looked to by common readers as their primary source of knowledge and wisdom about the world, so much so that it is tempting to call the era the Age of the Writer. Writers were respected as people who could convey incisive understanding and truth and wisdom about the world; novels, stories, poems, and plays were respected as "mirrors" of the actual. Journalists are sometimes said to write the "first rough drafts" of history. For many readers, fiction writers, poets, and playwrights wrote the second, third, and fourth drafts. "Ethnography," a word meaning "the scientific description of nations or races of men, with their customs, habits, and points of difference" was first used in the mid-nineteenth century, according to the *Oxford English Dictionary*; by the 1880s, an "ethnographer" was defined as a person who "studied the customs, the manners, the beliefs of men." Ethnography would later become the province of fields such as anthropology and sociology. But for a long time writers wrote the standard American ethnographies, relying not on scientific method, data collection, analysis, and peer review but on their own observations, intuitions, contextual knowledge, and ability to understand psychological and behavioral patterns. Writers had to do all this, it should be added, while entertaining or at least interesting readers and, furthermore, they had to do it while making money and creating glory for their publishers and for themselves.

To whom else could contemporary readers have turned for knowledge except writers, to whom else could they have listened? Radio and movies did not begin to fully develop until the 1920s, though a few earlier films, like *Birth of a Nation* (1915), taught major lessons to mass audiences. Mass newspapers and magazines were too rapidly produced and too tied to particular political and economic interests to be trusted as sources of truth and wisdom. The political writing issued by social change movements such as the Temperance movement and various left-wing radical movements sometimes commanded large audiences but tended toward formulaic redundancy. Academic disciplines and subjects such as sociology, history, political science, and business management did not begin to develop until the final decades of the nineteenth century, and in any case few common readers could have found much illumination in the language and methods of many professors. Writers, then, had little competition for the attention of the serious American reading audience.

That audience was not formally educated to a high or even moderate degree. Through much of the period, elementary school attendance up until age 12 or 13 was as much education as the great majority of individuals received; some immigrant groups as well as black Americans living in the South received substantially less. High school was for a select few: less than 2 percent of all 17-year-olds graduated from high school in 1870, about 6 percent graduated in 1900, about 16 percent graduated in 1920, and about 29 percent in 1930. College was for the *extremely* select few. In the last decades of the nineteenth century about 2 percent of people aged 18 to 24 were enrolled in colleges; by 1919, about 5 percent of that cohort was enrolled. Of course, formal education was not the only kind of education available. Lots of people, or at least lots of people who could actually read, were self-taught, and, according to many accounts, for them reading was *the* way to knowledge and wisdom. This is not to suggest that common readers, whether self-taught or formally educated, necessarily always turned to serious writing as opposed to "entertaining" and "light" writing. Nor is it to say that reading was high on the list of things to do for the great majority of Americans who worked, on average, 10 or 11 hours each day for five-and-one-half or six days each week, or who endlessly kept house and took care of children. But, to repeat the fundamental point, there was a substantial audience for serious writing, a substantial number of people who looked to writers as major sources of knowledge about the world.

A considerable amount of American writing produced in the 1865–1929 period is still read. Many writers have been translated into several, sometimes dozens of, foreign languages. Hundreds of thousands of US college students and thousands in other countries enroll each year in courses that provide broad surveys and specific courses focusing on particular writers, literary movements, and themes. Some US secondary students are also exposed to this writing. This is all good news. But much of the social content of the writing is lost on modern readers, including professional readers such as teachers and professors. The networks of detailing, the references to ways of thinking about issues, the complex interconnections of core issues – that is, the particular contexts – no longer make much sense to them. As a result, literary works are often ripped from their contexts and their meanings destroyed, their richness lessened.

The 1865 to 1929 era was tumultuous. There was the troubled aftermath of the Civil War, the Spanish–American War, and World War I. There were economic depressions in the 1870s and 1890s as the country was becoming the world's mightiest industrial economy. There were expositions and "world's fairs" that celebrated American power and know-how. There were great opportunities, great fortunes made, a significant increase in the number of people who were solidly middle class, and, always, great numbers of poor people. There were catastrophes like the burning of 12,000 build-ings on three square miles of Chicago in 1871, the destruction of much of San Francisco by earthquake and fire in 1906, and the deaths of more than half a million Americans (and tens of millions of others around the world) in the influenza pandemic of 1918. There was massive immigration until the 1920s and large migrations of populations within the country. Major scientific and technological breakthroughs reshaped the day-to-day lives of people and the ways business and work got done. Whole new cities arose and some old ones grew at rapid rates. The era had catastrophes at both ends, the bloody Civil War at the one end and the Great Depression at the other.

Writers do not usually write about historical events and patterns, demo-graphic shifts, natural or man-made catastrophes, and so forth. They do, however, sometimes without even knowing that they are doing it, write about the human impact of events, the particular feel and texture of history as experienced by their characters.

This book discusses the main, ongoing, disputed issues that are some-times directly and sometimes indirectly embedded in the classic literature of the 1865 to 1929 era. The goal of each chapter is to broadly describe the issue, then to suggest how the issue was involved in representative literary works. Several major themes and concerns run through the literature, just as they run through the history: (1) those involving the acceptance or exclusion of certain racial and ethnic minorities; (2) those focused on the uses of violence and mob action to achieve goals or as forms of self- or group-expression; (3) those focused on class conflict and the existence of great numbers of poor people and small numbers of rich people; (4) those involving efforts to fundamentally change things and to create a new, more equitable, more decent world; and (5) those involving assessments of whether the good and authentic American life was best lived in cities or in small towns and on farms.

The chapters in this book are not intended to be complete discussions of literary works but as relatively brief examples of how to read texts in their contexts. Nor are they intended to be histories, either in the sense that they represent what historians have learned about events and issues over time or in the sense that they summarize what *really*, objectively happened. Discussions of immigration at the turn of the twentieth century, for example, stressed sensational interethnic violence, the seeming impossibility of assimilating certain groups, and the emergence of some big cities as "alien" enclaves. Modern historians of immigration have far more complex, sophisticated analyses based on a far more impressive array of evidence than contemporaries possessed. Early twentieth-century public discourse about black Americans, to cite a second example, stressed their ignorance and abject circumstances, or, very infrequently, their victimization by whites. While certainly not denying that blacks were cruelly oppressed, modern historians of the black American experience have, among other things, recovered large bodies of neglected evidence, restored long-forgotten black voices, and discovered widespread indications that many blacks were active and successful agents of their own destinies.

Rather than being attempts at historical accuracy and completeness, the chapters describe how the issues might have been understood at the time by a curious, intelligent person – a smart writer, for example – who read considerably in contemporary sources including newspapers, magazines, nonfiction accounts, and so forth. Contemporary understandings of issues often tended toward stereotypes, prejudices, conventional wisdom, and unsupported generalizations. Some writers expressed those narrow understandings. Other writers broke free of them and represented the issues in fresh ways in their work, writing a different America for their readers. Not all major American writing of the era is accounted for in this book, I should add. Some writers were not attracted or were repelled by social issues. Others, among them a few of the most interesting – T. S. Eliot, Ezra Pound, and Gertrude Stein – left the US near the beginnings of their careers, resettled in Europe, and rarely wrote about life in America.

I should say a word about one aspect of the method I used in writing this book. Over many years, I have taught courses involving each of the subjects I have written about here and read a considerable body of historical literature. But to develop an understanding of how the writers experienced the unfolding events and their impacts on men and women – and, so to speak, to force the historical scholarship to the back of my mind – I also researched each subject in newspaper and magazine archives, in popular book discussions of the day, and in government publications. On a particular subject, I typically read hundreds of magazine and newspaper accounts and other documents. These formed, ultimately, the core of my discussions, especially in the opening chapters. So that readers can follow up and read for themselves, I usually only cite representative articles that appeared in newspapers like the *New York Times* and magazines like *Harper's* and *Atlantic* because they are relatively easy to access online and through libraries. On many subjects, I used as one of my primary resources the online database *C19: The Nineteenth Century Index* (which actually covers the period up until about 1920). Occasionally, I have also used relevant biographical details drawn from the authoritative online *American National Biography*. Also occasionally, I have cited contemporary reviews and commentaries on the literature to provide some insight into audience reactions and assessments.

1

Civil War Memories

The Context

The Civil War was the most painful, most horrific of human events to have ever taken place on US soil. By the accounting of the modern-day Department of Veterans Affairs, a combined total of 215,000 Confederate and Union soldiers died in combat, and an additional 283,000 died in noncombat situations. Close to 300,000 Union soldiers were wounded; Confederate nonmortal casualties were not estimated but were substantial. In the South, where much of the war was fought, there were significant civilian casualties and large areas that were devastated by the Union armies.

General Robert E. Lee surrendered the main Confederate army on April 9, 1865. Then, on April 14, President Lincoln was shot, dying the next day. People in the North were plunged into grief after only a few days of celebration of the war's end. People in the South also grieved, though there were some who saw Lincoln's death as providential or at least deserved.

The endings of wars sometimes lead to discussions of what the war meant, who did what, what troop movement or weapon determined the outcomes of particular battles, which leaders proved their mettle, what was heroic, who were heroes, and what were the immediate and long-term consequences of the war. From 1865 until the end of the century and beyond, there were widespread public discussions of the Civil War. Great numbers of publications poured out, including diaries, memoirs, biographies of generals, histories of regiments, books of battlefield photographs, and eyewitness accounts of battles. One of the most notable publications was the series of encyclopedic articles that appeared in monthly installments in *Century* magazine from November 1884 to November 1887. Written for the most part by former generals and focusing on the war's important battles and leaders, these articles, later collected in a four-volume set titled *Battles and Leaders of the Civil War*, should have satisfied even the most voracious readers of military history and lore.

A further indication of the war's effect on American society was the election to public office of men who had served with distinction. This was so at the municipal and state levels of government as well as at the national level. With the exception of Grover Cleveland, every President of the United States from Ulysses S. Grant, elected in 1868, through William McKinley, elected in 1896, was a high-ranking Union officer: Grant was the "General-in-Chief," Rutherford B. Hayes was a major general, James Garfield was a brigadier general, Chester Arthur was quartermaster general, Benjamin Harrison was a brigadier general, and McKinley was a major.

Memory of the war – which, like all human memory, was always and everywhere *selective* memory of the war – was kept alive in a number of other ways besides the election of old soldiers and writing of various kinds. Decoration Day, later called Memorial Day, the day on which the graves of fallen soldiers were decorated with flowers and mementos, began shortly after the end of the war and spread across the country over the next decades, with parades and speeches evolving to augment the graveside rites. In the 1880s and 1890s, spearheaded by veterans groups (the northern Grand Army of the Republic and the southern United Confederate Veterans), formal public remembrances of the war were widespread. Reenactments of battles were attended by thousands of people. Statues and war memorials were installed in virtually every city and county seat in the country. Banquets and other festive events were held in both North and South to commemorate particular battles.

The reconciliation of the North and the South was the major theme of most memorial events (slavery as a cause for the war and emancipation as a result were rarely mentioned). In what became a standard mode, aging veterans of both sides were reunited at battle sites where they were saluted in speeches as former heroic foes now joined in unending friendship. The September 1889 reunion of veterans of the Battle of Chickamauga, in northwestern Georgia, was typical. The *New York Times* for September 21, 1889 reported that 25,000 people were in attendance. The Governor of Georgia gave the major address, stressing that the country had overcome the old animosities and come together. In addition, the *Times* reported, General Rosencrans, who commanded the Union troops at Chickamauga, spoke "feelingly" of seeing before him old combatants sitting side by side and "engaging in pleasant, friendly converse."[1] Readers of such reports were, of course, encouraged to believe that the old soldiers were symbols for the healed, united, strong nation that had been formed after 1865.

The Literature

A great deal of anguished poetry concerning slavery and the war was published in magazines and newspapers in the years before it, during it, and immediately after the Civil War. Many important writers weighed in, including William Cullen Bryant, Ralph Waldo Emerson, Herman Melville, Henry Wadsworth Longfellow, John Greenleaf Whittier, Walt Whitman, and Frances Ellen Watkins Harper. No poem became as widely recited and sung as Julia Ward Howe's 1861 "The Battle Hymn of the Republic" or Charles C. Sawyer's 1862 "When This Cruel War Is Over," the most popular piece of sheet music produced during the war. In fact, much of the poetry was soon forgotten.

A few poets had some of their work remembered across generations. Poems such as Henry Timrod's "Ode: Sung on the Occasion of Decorating the Graves of the Confederate Dead" and Sidney Lanier's "The Dying Words of Jackson" continued to be read. Walt Whitman's 1865 elegy on the death of Lincoln, "When Lilacs Last in the Dooryard Bloom'd," came to be seen as iconic, and his later "O Captain, My Captain" was for many readers an even more important Lincoln poem. One impressive, long-forgotten poet who was recently rediscovered, Sarah Morgan Bryan Piatt, published a few remarkable war poems such as "A Hundred Years Ago" and "Army of Occupation: *At Arlington, 1866*."

Whitman was an enthusiastic advocate for the war when it began in 1861, writing a call to arms in "Beat! Beat! Drums!" Later, working in Washington as a volunteer hospital attendant to the northern wounded, moving among them, trying to see to their simple needs, writing letters for them, watching some of them die, he became considerably more sober. Poems in the 1866 *Drum-Taps*, which he continued to revise and augment until 1881, showed how profoundly he was changed by his hospital work. Some, like "A March in the Ranks Hard-Prest," "The Road Unknown," and "The Wound-Dresser," contained detailed descriptions of war's

---

[1] "The Blue and the Gray: Veterans of the War at a Battle Reunion," *New York Times*, September 21, 1889, p. 2.

horrors, including bullet wounds to the abdomen, a crushed head, an arm blown into a stump, a hand blown off, gangrene, and death spasms. "The Wound-Dresser" also included a confession by Whitman about how he had once urged "relentless war" and had then come among the "unsurpass'd heroes" of the war "to soothe them, or silently watch the dead." Such candor about patriotic excesses and such straightforward recognition of what happens to the frail human body when it is penetrated by bullets or ripped by bayonets were rare in Civil War writing before Whitman.

Whitman's *Specimen Days* (1881) included some 84 diary entries regarding his hospital work during the war. Anguished, sometimes astonished, he recorded case after case of the suffering of the wounded in language far more detailed and factual than his poems utilized. By providing the name of the wounded man, his army unit, the nature of his wound, and the prognosis, an entry like "Some Specimen Cases" was calculated to avoid abstractions about heroism. An entry like "Unnamed Remains the Bravest Soldier," on the other hand, recorded the lonely death of an anonymous soldier. "No formal general's report, nor book in the library, nor column in the paper, embalms the bravest, north or south, east or west," Whitman wrote. He completed the entry by remarking on how, standing for hundreds and thousands of others, the wounded "manliest" soldier crawls "aside to some bush-clump, or ferny tuft" and dies alone. His remains would not be discovered in the battlefield cleanup, and so "there at last, the Bravest Soldier crumbles in mother earth, unburied and unknown."

In the last entry of the *Specimen Days* series, titled "The Real War Will Never Get in the Books," Whitman remarked on the ways in which the war was then being remembered in the country. His frustration with human memory, or forgetfulness, was profound. "In the mushy influences of current times," he wrote, "the fervid atmosphere and typical events of those years are in danger of being totally forgotten." He ruled out the idea that the war could be properly understood through the "official surface courteousness of the Generals" or by studying what happened in battles. He dismissed the mythologizing of the war as a Grand Cause that had been underway almost since the first shot was fired.

As readers of his earlier work could have expected, Whitman was interested in the "actual soldier," the real combatant "with all his ways, his incredible dauntlessness, habits, practices, tastes, language, his fierce friendship, his appetite, rankness, his superb strength and animality, lawless gait. ..." But, sadly, Whitman believed that the war experienced by the "actual" soldiers would "never be written – perhaps must not and should not be." The "must not and should not" signaled Whitman's sense that writing about the real horror of the ordinary soldier's war would cross some line into prurient, undignified remembrance of the suffering of others.

The Civil War, as many scholars have remarked with some surprise, did not produce a great body of fiction. Some stories written by women were published during and just after the war, many of them set on the home front and focused on such themes as the domestic effects of men going off to war, the vital wartime responsibilities of women, and the role of women as encouragers of patriotic feeling in men who resisted service. With the exception of Louisa May Alcott's *Little Women* (1868), however, none of this popular fiction was read by later generations.

Then, in the late 1880s and 1890s, just as commemorations of the war were becoming very popular – and just as Realism was beginning to crest as a literary movement – a few writers published significant war fictions. Hamlin Garland's "The Return of a Private" was one of the stories in *Main-Travelled Roads* (1891) and, like every other story in that collection, it described the difficult lives of poor farm families in the upper Midwest. In it, Private Smith, recently discharged from the Union army, returned to his farm in western Wisconsin. No crowds cheered his three years of voluntary fighting for an "idea." Garland asserted that Private Smith had a "heroic soul" and was "a magnificent type," but his service did nothing for him. And so, Garland concluded, in a passage meant to apply to all the Private Smiths, "The common soldier of the American volunteer army had returned. His war with the South was over, and his fight, his daily running fight, with nature and against the injustices of his fellow men, was begun again."

Several years after Garland's story appeared, Harold Frederic published seven substantial Civil War home front stories set in the Mohawk Valley of New York, including "The Copperhead," "The Deserter," and "The War Widow." But, like much of Frederic's excellent fiction, these stories were rarely even mentioned in later years.

Virtually the only Civil War fiction that continued to be read by later generations was written by Ambrose Bierce and Stephen Crane. Crane was not born until 1871 and so had no experience of the war itself (he learned about it by reading books such as *Battles and Leaders of the Civil War*). Bierce, on the other hand, fought in a number of major engagements, including the very first battle of the war. He was severely wounded at Kennesaw Mountain, Georgia, recovered, and continued fighting until

January 1865. During his remarkable Union military career, Bierce received 15 commendations for "bravery under fire." He was an awesome soldier.

He was an awesome soldier who later became a fine San Francisco journalist and then, in the late 1880s, began to write fine fiction that on many occasions told the bitter, strange, violent stories of common soldiers caught up in surreal battles. Bierce was one of the age's great cynics, as many of the entries in his *Devil's Dictionary* suggested, and there was no way that he would have believed even for a moment in the country's feel-good memories of the Civil War as a collection of moments of glory, honor, sacrifice, and patriotism. His *Tales of Soldiers and Civilians* (1892) contained 13 stories, each of which had its own particular form of strangeness. Some involved the supernatural. Others, anticipating by decades some of the major innovations of modern narrative technique, highlighted weak connections between causes and effects, nonlinear structures, and the tensions between psychological and chronological time. The latter was demonstrated beautifully in the often reprinted "An Occurrence at Owl Creek Bridge." That story centered on the execution of a southern spy, but the hanging led to an escape narrative told from the point of view of the hanged man which ended only when the dead, hanging body came into view. Bierce had no interest in Realism, which he defined in his *Devil's Dictionary* as "The art of depicting nature as it is seen by toads. The charm suffusing a landscape painted by a mole, or a story written by a measuring-worm."

Many of the stories in *Tales of Soldiers and Civilians* went out of their way to highlight the terrible suffering and gruesome combat deaths experienced by soldiers. In "The Coup de Grace," for instance, a wounded soldier was attacked by swine; the narrator remarked that when one animal was through with the body, "The only visible wound was a wide, ragged opening in the abdomen. It was defiled with earth and dead leaves. Protruding from it was a loop of small intestine." In "An Affair of Outposts," a politician visited a battlefield and remarked in gentlemanly words, "this is beastly! Where is the charm of it all? Where are the elevated sentiments, the devotion, the heroism, the — ?"

"Chickamauga" became the most famous combat story of *Tales of Soldiers and Civilians*. Bierce knew the Battle of Chickamauga intimately, having been in it and having observed important elements of it as a Union battlefield mapmaker, and in later years he was to write about it on four other occasions. "Chickamauga" was published for the first time in the San Francisco *Examiner* on January 20, 1889, as the preparations for the September commemoration of the battle were underway. It was narrated for the most part from the point of view of a child who, we are told at the outset, carries within him the human race's desire for conquest and who had learned about battlefield postures of "aggression and defense" from picture books. Wandering from his home, the child witnessed a battle; watched as wounded men crawled through the forest; tried to ride a crawling soldier who threw him off and revealed that he was missing his lower jaw and "from the upper teeth to the throat was a great red gap fringed with hanging shreds of flesh and splinters of bone"; slept through another battle; led a parade of dying soldiers; and "danced with glee" when he got back to his own home and saw that everything was on fire. Then he noticed a dead woman, apparently his mother, her "white face turned upward, the hands thrown out and clutched full of grass, the clothing deranged, the long dark hair in tangles and full of clotted blood." As if this did not go far enough, Bierce added a flourish saying that "The greater part of her forehead was torn away and from the jagged hole the brain protruded, over-flowing the temple, a frothy mass of gray, crowned with clusters of crimson bubbles – the work of a shell." Complete with the mockery of seemingly innocent "frothy" gray matter and "crimson bubbles," the passage, like the story itself, seemed calculated to end any idea of celebrating war and to make impossible the idea of romantic, sweet combat death. One wonders what the aging warriors who gathered at Chickamauga a few months after its publication would have thought about it. Would the former combatants have continued to engage in "pleasant, friendly converse," as General Rosencrans was said to have observed on that occasion?

Detailed accounts of gruesome wounds, sudden deaths, and slow deaths also abound in Stephen Crane's combat novel, *The Red Badge of Courage* (1895). But Crane was most intent in that novel on, first, describing and analyzing the battlefield behavior of his protagonist, Private Henry Fleming, and, second, assessing the role of memory and forgetfulness in the composition of Fleming's ultimate character.

As with the child in "Chickamauga," one of the key elements of Fleming's preparation was his learning of war stories: before he volunteered for service, he had dreamed of "vague and bloody conflicts that had thrilled him with their sweep and fire," he "had imagined peoples secure in the shadow of his eagle-eyed prowess," and "had read of marches, sieges, conflicts, and he had longed to see it all." Through his education, he had no doubt also absorbed one of the era's fundamental concepts, that an individual could develop a "character," a set of values that would not change no matter what circumstances he faced, no matter how brutally he was assaulted. That idea underlay conventional definitions of heroism – the war hero was the man of character who in combat continued to demonstrate his steadfast commitment to concepts like self-sacrifice and honor and patriotism.

Private Fleming feared that he might prove to be a coward. But he performed well in his first combat and, furthermore, in a good sign that he could put aside romantic, literary notions of war, he noticed that "There was a singular absence of heroic poses" among the combatants and that "The officers, at their intervals, rearward, neglected to stand in picturesque attitudes." But then, facing a second charge by the enemy, he and some of his fellow soldiers, frightened and horrified, threw down their arms and ran away.

The Red Badge of Courage, which takes place over a two-day period, is almost entirely focused on Private Fleming's consciousness as it is bombarded by intense events, battle scenes, images of gruesome wounds, and deaths. Through this focus, Crane undercuts the notion that an individual can retain a steadfast "character" during combat: Fleming's behavior is shown to be the consequence not of self-mastery or will or belief or values but of irrational fear and animalistic hatred. In his first battle, Crane remarks, he fought well because he fell into a "red rage" and "developed the acute exasperation of a pestered animal, a well-meaning cow worried by dogs." He ran during his second battle because he exaggerated the enemy's prowess and also because soldiers near him ran. Later, Private Fleming rejoins his brigade and fights well. Why? What has changed? Did he rededicate himself to steadfastness of character? No. He fights well because he goes completely outside of himself, as evidenced by "the chaos of his brain" and the "glazed vacancy of his eyes." And, in spite of the fact that he has no self, no "character," or because of this fact, he is now seen by his comrades as a "war devil" and a "hero."

Crane examined not just how and why his protagonist behaved in combat but how he remembered and revised his memories of his behavior. While Fleming had in fact volunteered for service because of his interest in experience and because of a "prolonged ecstasy of excitement" about serving, as Crane indicated early in the novel, under the pressure of combat he revises his motivations and maintains that "he never wished to come to the war," that "he had been dragged by the merciless government" into service. Why had he deserted? In fact, he deserted because he exaggerated the abilities of the enemy and saw his comrades running, according to the details provided in the desertion scene. Later, though, Private Fleming revises the cause of his desertion – not once, but three times. In his first revision, he remembers that he saved himself to aid the army and had thus "proceeded according to very correct and commendable rules." Later, sensing the impending defeat of the Union army, he claims in his second revision that his running would prove to be "a roundabout vindication of himself." Still later, after he has proven himself in battle, he comments on other men running and revises the cause of his desertion a third time, now remembering that he himself "had fled with discretion and dignity." What do these "memories" of the same event have in common? Only the principle that the remembrance of an event is shaped by current circumstances and the need for self-promotion.

Nearly all of *The Red Badge of Courage* occurs in the rapidly unfolding present, and so, aside from Fleming's revisions of his reasons for running and a few moments when he thinks of his home, memory is not a dominant motif. But near the end of the novel, as the battles are finished and time slows down, the roles of memory and forgetfulness become prominent. At the end of Chapter 21, Fleming and a comrade are told by another soldier that two officers had been heard discussing how well they fought. After a few moments of embarrassment, Crane wrote, "They speedily forgot many things. The past held no pictures of error and disappointment. They were very happy, and their hearts swelled with grateful affection for the colonel and the youthful lieutenant." Two sentences later, ironically "cured" of bad memories by forgetfulness, Fleming now "felt supreme self-confidence."

Nationally, the Civil War evolved in the 1880s and 1890s into rosy memories, driven by historical revisionism, that were manifested in parades and statues and oratory. In the last chapter of *The Red Badge of Courage*, Crane used the language of Civil War commemorative parades in describing how Fleming now contemplated a "procession of memory" complete with lively music celebrating his battle deeds: "He spent delightful minutes viewing the gilded images of memory." This was a way of saying that the same national, social processes of memory that transformed a gruesome war into something beautiful were present in the mind of an ordinary soldier even as the war was being fought. Who was Fleming at the end? A person whose self consisted of imaginative concoctions, half-truths, and outright falsehoods. Who or what was the nation as a result of *its* selective memory? Crane did not say, though I think that it is fair to conclude that he was not impressed with the nation's sense of accuracy or its steadfastness of vision.

Some contemporary reviewers applauded Crane's understanding of war and appreciated its originality. William Dean Howells, for instance, writing in *Harper's Weekly* in October, 1895, commented on how Crane conveyed "the sense of deaf and blind turmoil," the "cloud of bewilderment" that soldiers experience during battle.[2] One British reviewer, George Wyndham, in the January 1896 *New Review*, remarked that Crane's novel was as good as Leo Tolstoy's *War and Peace* (1869) or Emile Zola's *The Downfall* (1892) and claimed that Crane was the innovator of a new device, the recording of the successive impressions made on Private Henry "from minute to minute during two days of heavy fighting."[3] An anonymous British reviewer, writing in the *Spectator* in June, 1896, suggested that Crane's book was a fine novel and, also, "an interesting and painful essay in pathology" that precisely charted the effects of danger in modern warfare "upon the human nervous system."[4]

The two British reviewers were exactly right, I think. So far as I know, *The Red Badge of Courage* is the first American fiction to present in such detail the minute-by-minute experience of a person undergoing intense experiences. So far as I know, too, it is the first extended narration – though some of the stories in Bierce's *Tales of Soldiers and Civilians* were, arguably, brief examples of the type – to depict combat as the pathological clash of overly stimulated nervous systems.

[2] William Dean Howells, "Review of *The Red Badge of Courage*," *Harper's Weekly*, 39 (October 26, 1895), p. 1013.
[3] George Wyndham, "A Remarkable Book," *New Review*, 14 (January 1896), pp. 30–40.
[4] Anon., "Review," *Spectator*, 76 (June 27, 1896), pp. 924–6.

2

"A Serfdom of Poverty and Restricted Rights"
Black Americans after Emancipation

The Context

In April 1865, when the Civil War finally ended, conditions were grim in the 11 states which had formed the Confederacy. The physical damage wrought by the Union armies was severe. The economy was shattered.

Even before the war ended, Lincoln and his fellow Republicans had begun to consider what needed to be done to rebuild the South, and a long series of questions emerged. How would the Confederate states be readmitted to the Union? How would state and local governments be established? Would there be amnesty for those who fought for the Confederacy? Would former Confederate soldiers, officers, and politicians vote in elections? Would the aristocrats who led the prewar South, the plantation owners, be the postwar leaders? How would the economy be rebuilt? And, most importantly, would former slaves be able to work as free men and women and would they get political and civil rights?

In time, many of the fundamental questions were addressed, more or less. But not, except momentarily, those pertaining to the rights of former slaves. From 1865 to 1876, during the Reconstruction period, those issues became the subject of a fierce political tug-of-war in Washington and in southern cities and the southern countryside. After Reconstruction ended, the circumstances of southern blacks deteriorated sharply.

Some politicians, led by so-called Radical Republicans who sought fundamental change in the South, were occasionally successful because of their abilities at political deal making and coalition building, with the result that some Reconstruction legislation was passed that promised, over time, to dramatically improve the circumstances of southern blacks. A number of black colleges were established during Reconstruction. Black men were given the vote by the Fifteenth Amendment to the Constitution and exercised it to the advantage of their people. Some black men were elected to public office and many performed with distinction. Northern educators, working under the aegis of the Freedman's Bureau, moved into the South and, sometimes joined by enlightened southern whites, began educating the black masses.

Southern Democratic politicians and their constituents, while conceding that slavery had indeed ended, fought hard against every effort to extend political and civil rights to blacks and made every possible effort to insure that blacks continued to exist in complete, slave-like subordination to whites. Political resistance to Reconstruction in the chambers of Congress and in southern state capitals was generally through debate and parliamentary maneuvering. On the ground, in southern cities and in the countryside, resistance to black rights was direct and violent.

Some resistance from southern diehards had been anticipated, and the Federal government therefore kept troops stationed in the South after the war. They were expected to perform police and judicial duties when necessary, to oversee dysfunctional or resisting local governments, and to respond to any outbreaks of violence. The army area of operation stretched from the Mason–Dixon Line south to the Gulf of Mexico and from the Atlantic coast west to Texas, a vast expanse. But, perversely, as southern resistance to black rights mounted, the size of the Federal occupation forces declined. In 1865, there were 202,000 troops stationed across the 11 former Confederate states. Six months later, there were 88,000. From 1868 until 1876, there were 11,000. The army was, needless to say, stretched thin.

In 1866, the first riots against the extension of rights to blacks took place in April in Norfolk, Virginia; in May in Memphis, Tennessee; and in July and August in New Orleans, Louisiana. The Memphis riots included extensive fighting between black soldiers who were part of the Federal Army and the predominately Irish local police force. The New Orleans riots were reported in newspapers to be a reaction by outraged citizens to a "revolutionary" political convention of freedmen and their northern white leaders. The August 5, 1866 *New York Times* contained a lengthy article providing a reporter's eyewitness account of the fierce, blood-soaked battles that were fought in the vicinity of Canal Street, a report on the martial law declaration, and reprints of local press reports. The reprint from the *New Orleans Times* reported the story the way that southern newspapers would essentially report all riot or "massacre" stories over the next decade, that is, as the proper and righteous repulsion of revolution by peace-loving whites. "A band of poor, deluded negroes, urged on by unprincipled white men" had attacked whites, the paper said, continuing:

> Armed with pistols, clubs and razors, they collected in great numbers around the Mechanics' Institute, for the avowed purpose of defending the revolutionary Jacobins who had raised the terror of negro suffrage, and the result of their folly is sorrowfully apparent. Left to themselves, the negroes never would have joined in a treasonable scheme to overthrow the State Government; but they listened to the words of the tempters, and into the pit dug for others they have fallen.[1]

Direct resistance by whites continued into the 1870s. The largest anti-black riots occurred at Colfax, Mississippi, in 1873; at Vicksburg, Mississippi, New Orleans and Coushatta, Louisiana, in 1874; at Yazoo City and Clinton, Mississippi, in 1875; and at Hamburg, South Carolina, in 1876. The Louisiana "massacres" and riots were the subject of considerable commentary in the northern press, as in a *New York Times* February 1875 article which reported on the testimony taken from army officers and police, and a September 1874 article about the Coushatta events.[2] Coming as it did near the end of Reconstruction, and involving the cold-blooded executions of a number of blacks, the Hamburg, SC massacre was more widely reported and discussed than the earlier incidents. It also provoked a widely published letter from President Grant to the Governor of South Carolina. The President wrote:

> The scene at Hamburg, as cruel, bloodthirsty, wanton, unprovoked, and uncalled for as it was, is only a repetition of the course which has been pursued in other Southern States within the last few years, notably in Mississippi and Alabama. Mississippi is governed to-day by officials chosen through fraud and violence such as would scarcely be accredited to savages, much less to a civilized and Christian people.[3]

---

[1] "The Riot in New-Orleans," *New York Times*, August 5, 1866, p. 5.

[2] "The Louisiana Outrages: Proceedings Before the Investigating Committee," *New York Times*, February 3, 1875, p. 5; "The Southern Terror," *New York Times*, September 10, 1874, p. 7.

[3] "The Hamburg Butchery.; – Communication to the Senate. Correspondence of the President with Gov. Chamberlain – The Course of the Latter Concurred in, and All Necessary and to Punish the Murderers Promised," *New York Times*, August 2, 1876, p. 5.

Some riots may have been spontaneous, but secret organizations whose goals were to keep blacks in their place – the membership was kept secret because they were participating in illegal activities – sprung up across the South. White Leagues existed in hundreds of communities. Founded in 1866, the Ku Klux Klan was the most famous of the secret resistance groups. The KKK had clear strategic goals and a set of well-developed terror tactics that included cross burnings, beatings, and ritual murder of outspoken blacks and, sometimes, their white supporters. It portrayed its resistance to black rights as biblical, Christian, and moral.

Northern support for black rights was tepid. There was no Congressional support for an expanded military presence in the South, even when the Republicans were in the majority. Furthermore, the North had its own problems in the 1870s. In 1871, a fire that burned much of the business core of Chicago led to the failures of some major insurance companies and banks and to a stock market crash. In 1873, there was a financial panic that led to a major depression. Scandals involving Congressional Republicans as well as big city northern Democrats were distractions. Union agitation in the manufacturing and mining sectors increased yearly. Urban riots involving Irish Catholics absorbed a good deal of attention. There was also considerable Congressional and Army pressure for Federal troops to be redeployed from the South to the West, where they were needed to help prosecute the Indian wars. Finally, in 1876, the Presidential election was so close that Republicans had to make a deal with southern Democrats in order to salvage the election for their candidate, Rutherford B. Hayes. The deal was that southern Democrats would support the election of Hayes in the Electoral College if Republicans pledged to end their support for Reconstruction. The pledge was made.

The long-running Indian Wars were another major indication of how miserably and unjustly people of color were treated in the US. Takeovers of Native American lands, treaties established and broken by State and Federal governments, genocides committed against tribes, and murders that went unpunished were routine occurrences. According to the Department of Veterans Affairs, some 1,000 US troops were killed between 1817 and 1898 in the Indian Wars (250 at General Custer's Battle of the Little Bighorn in 1876). That was a tiny fraction of Native American deaths. Helen Hunt Jackson, the author of *A Century of Dishonor* (1881), coauthor of the government-commissioned *Report on the Conditions and Needs of the Mission Indians* (1883), and author of the popular novel *Ramona* (1884), wrote penetrating accounts of this history of cruel mistreatment;

other reports appeared frequently. But the exposés fell on deaf ears, while the Native American population continued to decline (from 339,000 in 1860 to 248,000 in 1890) and to become increasingly troubled. In the next chapter, I will comment on the US treatment of Chinese during this same period.

After 1876, it did not take long for both informal and legal devices insuring southern black subservience to be developed. The vote given to black men by the Fifteenth Amendment could not be undone. But in the late 1870s southern states began to impose literacy requirements on blacks (a demonstration of reading and writing abilities, sometimes at sophisticated levels) as a prerequisite for voting and, as well, a tax to be paid on election day by any black seeking to vote. These requirements made it extremely difficult for a black man to exercise his rights. Further, a series of court cases at both the state and Federal levels found that the segregation of public facilities was legal. In 1883, the Supreme Court of the United States declared unconstitutional the Civil Rights Act of 1875, which had prohibited segregation. In 1896, the Court found in the case of *Plessy v. Ferguson* that separate but equal facilities were Constitutional; in 1899, the "separate but equal" doctrine was specifically applied by the Court to educational facilities. Other laws prohibited marriage between the races, quantified how much black blood defined legal blackness, and so forth. The various segregation laws, known generally as "Jim Crow" laws, continued in effect past the middle of the twentieth century.

The legal superstructure of segregation was one element of the return of southern blacks to near-slavery conditions. Blacks also continued to be terrorized, deprived of economic opportunities, relegated to low status and poorly paid employment, and deprived of education. Antiblack riots occurred frequently in both the South and the North. Between 1898 and 1915, the largest and most deadly were in Wilmington, North Carolina, in 1898; in southern Illinois in 1898 and 1899; in New Orleans and New York City in 1900; in Joplin, Missouri, in 1903; in Springfield, Illinois, in 1904; in Springfield, Missouri, Chattanooga, Tennessee, Greensburg, Indiana, Brownsville, Texas, and Atlanta, Georgia, in 1906; in Springfield, Illinois (again!) in 1908; in 11 different cities in 1910 following the victory of black boxer Jack Johnson over James Jeffries in a heavyweight championship fight; and in Palestine, Texas, in 1911. Full accounts of those race riots are available in Rucker and Upton's *Encyclopedia of American Race Riots*.[4] Riots

---

[4] Walter Rucker and James Nathaniel Upton, *Encyclopedia of American Race Riots*, 2 vols (Greenwood Press, Westport, CT, 2007).

involving immigrants and riots between immigrant groups were also frequent in late nineteenth- and early twentieth-century America, as I shall detail in the next chapter. It was an unruly, sometimes murderous, time in American history, though no group suffered as much as blacks.

Lynching, the killing without legal sanction of an alleged offender by self-constituted executioners, occurred with great frequency. By one count, 3,436 people were lynched in the United States between 1889 and 1922, an average of more than 100 each year; the number of lynchings that took place between 1889 and 1960 was 4,700. Whites were sometimes the victims, and the largest mass lynching took place in New Orleans in 1891, when 11 Italian immigrants, who had just been acquitted of the murder of the police commissioner, were pulled out of jail by a mob led by the New Orleans district attorney, then shot or hung. But by far the greatest number of lynch victims were black. Many lynchings were public spectacles, bringing out large numbers of people who heckled the condemned, watched his painful death, made jokes, and, on some occasions, helped to dismember him and to pass out souvenir parts and bones.

Lynching was attacked on legal and moral grounds as unjust, inhumane, disgusting, and so forth. There were, on the other hand, standard public defenses of it. A good example of such a standard defense was contained in a letter to the editor of the magazine *The Outlook* in October 1893. The writer, J. J. D. of Lebanon, Tennessee, argued that courts sometimes took too long to mete out justice and thus caused impatient people to rise up. He also said that southerners were trying to educate blacks. Educational reform could be expected to take place, but slowly. In the meantime, he asked, "Are we … to submit to outrages committed by the thousands of [black] brutes who are beyond the reach of education?" Telling people to stop lynching others was impossible: "It is as useless to advise the South against lynching as [it is to advise] the North against strikes. It is a condition which brings about these evils, and they will continue until the condition is removed." The writer concluded by suggesting black misbehavior caused lynching. Enslaved blacks had been "under the direction and moral influence of their masters," and, in fact, "The most industrious, peaceable, and moral of the negroes are those who were reared as slaves." Now, though, there was no moral compass for blacks. Lynching, then, provided black beasts with a moral compass.[5]

A decade after J. J. D expressed himself, a "Southern white woman" interviewed in 1905 by the *Independent* magazine as part of a series of

---

[5] J. J. D., "A Defense of Lynching," *Outlook*, 48 (October 28, 1893), p. 778.

portraits of "undistinguished" Americans, spoke about the "negro's innate vulgarity," the idea of the "educated negro" as not fitting "our natural order," and the negro's "degenerate nature." She also spoke about the good work done by the KKK in submitting the negro to necessary "drastic training," the criminality of negro men which was the cause of lynching, and the fake virtue that negroes often expressed and that naïve northerners in particular might mistake for reality.[6] Hers were standard southern attitudes.

The reference of the "Southern white woman" to the good work done by the KKK was part of a long effort to explain that organization as a force for morality and decency. Typical of that effort was D. L. Wilson's article published in the July 1884 *Century* magazine, which maintained that the Klan was really a benign organization but that some people, acting in its name, may have committed excesses from time to time. But, then, the author said, during Reconstruction the South had been in a state of revolution: white scum had been thrown to the top of society by the agitation of blacks, many of whom behaved as if they had been freed "from the common and ordinary obligations of citizenship." That is why the Klan stepped in. "Without it," the author said, "life to decent people would not have been tolerable."[7]

In 1890, some 7.6 million people, 12 percent of the American population of 62.2 million, were listed by the US Census Bureau as "colored." About 90 percent of them lived in the old Confederate states. The great masses of those southern blacks faced desperate times. Were the situations of northern blacks different? How did they fare in the farmlands and small towns of the North, the Midwest, and the West? There were no contemporary answers to this question. How did they fare in northern cities with expanding economies? The first attempt to systematically answer this question began in the mid-1890s, when W. E. B. DuBois, the great black scholar, began his extensive door-to-door surveys of the black population of Philadelphia. Using the most modern empirical methods and statistical analysis, Dr. DuBois published *The Philadelphia Negro: A Social Study* in 1899. Philadelphia then had a relatively substantial population compared to most northern cities (3.8% of the total population of 1 million, or

---

[6]   A Southern White Woman, "Experiences of the Race Problem," *Independent*, 56 (March 17, 1904), pp. 590–5.
[7]   D. L. Wilson, "The Ku Klux Klan: Its Origin, Growth, and Disbandment," *Century Illustrated Magazine*, 28 (July 1884), pp. 398–411.

38,000). A significant majority lived in the Seventh Ward in the central city, close to manufacturing, service, and construction jobs, close to municipal services, and within a few blocks of the mansions of millionaires on Rittenhouse and Washington Squares. But Philadelphia's blacks were nonetheless doing poorly, according to DuBois. Ninety percent of black men and women, when they were able to find work at all, were employed as domestic servants and laborers and were not given other opportunities in the job market; illiteracy and crime rates were high; there was overcrowding and poor sanitation in black neighborhoods.

DuBois also published a series of four articles in the *New York Times Magazine* in late 1901 in which he analyzed the situation of northern blacks. DuBois's thesis was that "North as well as south, the negroes have emerged from slavery into a serfdom of poverty and restricted rights." The two New York City articles which began the series noted the severe strains under which black "immigrants" from the South struggled. Perhaps two-thirds of New York's 60,000 blacks were decent working people who had been condemned to a narrow range of job opportunities by racism. Perhaps one-third were members of the "vicious and criminal classes" because membership in those classes was exactly the logical result of poor material circumstances, few opportunities, and general "oppression." The Philadelphia article, the third in the series, boiled down the results of DuBois's book-length study of that city. The Boston article that ended the series gave readers some hope. Boston's relatively small black population had progressed toward inclusion and accomplishment, DuBois said, because the way upward had been opened by progressive white attitudes.[8]

How black Americans could progress was widely debated. Through the last two decades of the nineteenth century, Booker T. Washington had been recognized by whites as well as most blacks as the spokesman for black Americans. The founder of Tuskegee Institute in Alabama, a prominent lecturer, and a man with an extensive network of powerful friends, Washington promoted vocational education for blacks, which he defined as education aimed at the achievement of "brains, property, and character." Faced with continuing assaults by whites on blacks, Washington

[8] W. E. B. DuBois, "The Black North; A Social Study: New York City, *New York Times*, November 17, 1901, p. SM10 and November 24, 1901, p. SM11; "The Black North; A Social Study: Philadelphia," *New York Times*, December 1, 1901, p. SM11; "The Black North; A Social Study: Boston," *New York Times*, December 8, 1901, p. SM20.

counseled patience, did not challenge the "separate but equal" doctrine, and generally struck an "accomodationist" tone. Blacks, according to Washington, would have to first earn the respect of whites; political and social equality would come later. In his famous "Atlanta Compromise" speech of 1895, he said that "The wisest among my race understand that the agitation of questions of social equality is the extremest folly, and that progress in the enjoyment of all the privileges that will come to us must be the result of severe and constant struggle rather than of artificial forcing." In what was clearly an endorsement of segregation, Washington said: "In all things that are purely social we can be as separate as the fingers, yet one as the hand in all things essential to mutual progress."[9] In the years following the "Atlanta Compromise" speech, Washington was embraced by powerful white people, including Presidents William McKinley and Theodore Roosevelt. Roosevelt had Washington to dinner at the White House in 1901, which produced a great deal of outrage among whites across the country.

W. E. B. DuBois and other prominent blacks looked upon Washington's "accomodationist" stance with increasing disfavor after 1900. In the chapter titled "On Mr. Booker T. Washington and Others" in his 1903 *The Souls of Black Folk*, DuBois accused Washington of leading blacks into "submission" and argued that what blacks had gotten in return for their submission was disenfranchisement, civil inferiority, and "the steady withdrawal of aid from institutions for the higher training of the Negro."[10] In 1903, DuBois published "The Talented Tenth," an article arguing that black progress could only come from the top echelons of black society, from the leadership of "exceptional men" who had received advanced education, not the sort of vocational education that Washington and others championed. This article echoed one by the Reverend H. L. Morehouse titled "The Talented Tenth" which had appeared in the *Independent* in April 1896.[11] Morehouse was associated with the Atlanta Baptist College, which changed its name to Morehouse College in 1913 in tribute to him.

---

[9]   Booker T. Washington, "Atlanta Compromise" speech, available at http://historymatters. gmu.edu/d/39/.

[10]   W. E. B. DuBois, "Of Mr. Booker T. Washington and Others," in *Souls of Black Folk* (A. C. McClurg, Chicago, 1903), pp. 50–5.

[11]   W. E. B. DuBois, "The Talented Tenth," from *The Negro Problem: A Series of Articles by Representative Negroes of To-day* (James Pott, New York, 1903), pp. 33–75; H. L. Morehouse, "The Talented Tenth," *Independent*, 48 (April 23, 1896), p. 1.

Discussions among blacks about strategies by which to secure equality, civil rights, and economic power would continue for decades. The earliest initiatives to flow from those discussions were the Niagara Movement, founded in 1904, and the National Association for the Advancement of Colored People, founded in 1909 after the riot in Springfield, Illinois. Both militantly advocated for civil and political rights, and in both DuBois played a central role.

White attitudes towards blacks evolved at a snail's pace, as was amply demonstrated in March 1915, when D. W. Griffith's film *The Birth of a Nation* premiered in New York. The film's first showing and its subsequent screenings to rave reviews was, in effect, the opening ceremony in the country's celebration of the 50th anniversary of the end of the Civil War. Like the celebration, the film stressed the reconciliation of North and South and the strength of the nation. It did this by retelling the southern version of the Reconstruction story. Reconstruction, according to captions within the silent *The Birth of a Nation*, was fomented by maddened northern "radicals" who wanted to "punish the South and hang their leaders." Ignorant blacks were given the vote while it was taken from whites. Deep-seated, bestial black male desire for white women was enabled by legislation passed by black politicians that permitted the "intermarriage of blacks and whites." "Crazed negroes" oppressed "helpless whites." The result was that "degradation and ruin" and "anarchy" was rampant across the South. How had the South overcome the "crazed negroes"? White men had formed the heroic, chivalric Ku Klux Klan and then, under its inspirational leadership, the white population rose up in "defense of their Aryan birthright."

Between its graphic battle scenes, its images of bestial blacks, wholesome whites, and heroic Klansman, *The Birth of a Nation* also provided its viewers with quotations from scholars who supported its interpretation of Reconstruction. Much of this support came from *A History of the American People*, written by President Woodrow Wilson in 1902, when he was Professor of History at Princeton University. Included were Wilson's remarks about how blacks had been manipulated by northern "Adventurers," how there had been "a veritable overthrow of civilization in the South" by blacks and northerners, and how, finally, through the "instinct of self-preservation," "there had sprung into existence a great Ku Klux Klan, a veritable empire of the South, to protect the southern country." In effect, Wilson's words provided the film with a Presidential endorsement.

There were some calls for censoring it, and actual suppression of its showing in Ohio, but *The Birth of a Nation* delighted large audiences across the country. In terms of its interpretation of Reconstruction, the bestial nature of blacks, the motives behind race-mixing, and the duties of whites, it was not at all ground-breaking. Rather, it merely repeated all the old simplifications of Reconstruction history perpetrated by opponents and all the old, sad, almost universally accepted stereotypes about the nature of black men and women.

The Literature

Arguably, the most famous late nineteenth-century white southern writer, Joel Chandler Harris, humanized blacks in his *Uncle Remus* tales. But Harris's blacks, reflecting the southern understanding of the alleged benefits of slavery, were pre-emancipation people who existed happily and harmoniously on plantations. In northern white writing of the 1865 to 1920 period, blacks scarcely existed except as occasionally glimpsed waiters, laborers, and domestic servants. That probably reflected the fact that few blacks lived outside the South and were therefore simply unknown to northern writers. On occasion, however, some of the most important of these writers depicted black characters in some detail or otherwise remarked on blacks.

The conventional racist view of the era – that blacks were comic figures or beasts – was not usually challenged in what would later become standard literary works. A comically simple-minded, childlike, poorly spoken black, for instance, was described in Theodore Dreiser's *The Financier* (1912) as "tall, shambling, illiterate, [and] nebulous-minded." He had stolen a small pipe worth 25 cents and appeared in the novel's central court scene as comic relief when the financier Frank Cowperwood was being sentenced to prison. Similarly, a depiction of black men as beasts appeared in Upton Sinclair's *The Jungle* (1906). During a strike, black workers were used to replace white workers. They were given whiskey and women so that "there were stabbings and shootings, rape and murder stalking abroad." Sinclair claimed that "young white girls from the country" rubbed elbows with "big buck negroes with daggers in their boots" and, later, in displays such as "never before were witnessed in America, and never in the world since the days of Baal and Moloch" there were seen the "bodies of men and women, black and white, sleeping together, and as the women were the dregs from the brothels of Chicago, and the men were for the most part ignorant country negroes, the nameless diseases of vice were soon rife." This language is quoted from the original serialized version of the novel; in its trade edition, Sinclair toned it down a bit. But both the original and the expurgated descriptions at least equaled the worst contained in the most famous popular racist novel of the day, Thomas F. Dixon, Jr's *The Clansman* (1905), the book on which *The Birth of a Nation* was based. Unlike Dixon, though, Sinclair claimed to be, and was celebrated, as a progress-minded, democratic, socialist humanitarian.

Did any white writers of the 1865 to 1920 period produce any work which attempted to convey the humanity of black people? The most sustained attempt was Mark Twain's *The Adventures of Huckleberry Finn* (1885), in which the slave Jim (the novel is set in the 1850s) emerges as a decent, loving, sensitive human being, despite the fact that every other character with whom he is involved – including Huck Finn, until his partial awakening – abuses him, caricatures him, or treats him as a thing which only has value as a commodity. Twain probably knew slavery better than any other important white writer of the period. He grew up in Hannibal, Missouri, and set the beginning of *Huck Finn* there. In the 1850s, about a quarter of the residents of the Missouri county in which Hannibal was located owned slaves; many others, including Twain's family, rented slaves from their owners. He knew the various black dialects as well as anyone. He was also attentive to Reconstruction events and the beginnings of Jim Crow. All of that knowledge can be felt in the novel, as can the varieties of dumb, hateful, white belief about blacks. In fact, one of the primary things that makes Jim a positive character is that virtually everyone else is so inhumane, violent, murderous, stupid, besotted, duplicitous, self-absorbed, or, in the case of Huck himself, very slow to awaken to even an incomplete moral sense.

Twain's interest in black Americans continued. In 1901, he wrote an essay titled "The United States of Lyncherdom" in which he remarked on a report published in the *Chicago Tribune* about a recent surge of lynchings. In 1900, there had been 150 cases, by mid-1901 there had already been 88 cases. More than half of the lynchings occurred in Georgia, Alabama, Louisiana, and Mississippi, but, Twain noted, lynchings had recently spread to Colorado, California, Indiana, and Kansas. Twain also remarked on how lynching was often a community affair: "When there is a lynching the people hitch up [their wagons] and come miles to see it, bringing their wives and children." But while others had remarked on how lynchings often served as entertainments, especially in entertainment-starved rural areas, and often included the dismemberment of burned corpses so that the local folk could take home a souvenir of a bone or two, Twain asked why people really came out for these gruesome events. "Really to see it?" he asked. "No, they come only because they are afraid to stay at home, lest it be noticed and offensively commented upon." He called this "Moral cowardice," which he said was the "commanding feature" of 9,999 out of every 10,000 men. He concluded "The United States of Lyncherdom" with the observation that great numbers of American Christian missionaries were in China trying to convert the Chinese and suggested that they come home to work with the lynchers and their sympathizers.[12]

Unfortunately, Twain chose not to publish his essay, which he thought might be the introduction to a book on the history of lynching, because if he did, he said, "I shouldn't have even half a friend down there [in the South], after it issued from a press." Ironically, this sounded like an example of the "moral cowardice" he had written about.

Aside from Twain, the one other important turn-of-the-twentieth-century writer who wrote in a sustained way about blacks was Gertrude Stein. "Melanctha," the longest of the narratives in *Three Lives* (1909), told the story of a "half white," attractive, sensitive, very bright woman, focusing at length on her difficult relationship with a young doctor. In terms of how Melanctha's psychological life and her voice were rendered, the story was brilliant and innovative. But for readers unschooled in the motives and devices of early experimental Modernism, it presented vast challenges. In any case, very few copies of *Three Lives* were actually sold at the time of its first publication, though in later years, among some sophisticated readers, "Melanctha" became something of a Modernist classic.

Stein's Melanctha explains her world and lives her life through her "feelings." Similarly, Twain's Jim explains events mostly by reference to magical transformations, as when Huck reports that "Jim said the witches bewitched him and put him in a trance, and rode him all over the state," and by interpreting signs, symbols, and dreams, as in his lengthy discussion at the end of Chapter 8. But in terms of their "prerational" or "nonscientific" outlooks, neither Jim nor Melanctha is different from the white characters in their respective books. Anna and Lena, the two other women whose stories are recounted in *Three Lives*, see the world in terms parallel to Melanctha's. Huck, Tom Sawyer, and most other white characters in *Huckleberry Finn* are controlled by their superstitions, alcohol consump-

---

[12] Mark Twain, "The United States of Lyncherdom," available at http://people.virginia.edu/~sfr/enam482e/lyncherdom.html

tion, greed, animus, mob psychology, anger, and so forth. Rational thought is in very short supply in these, as in many other, American fictions of the era, regardless of race or ethnicity or social class or gender.

How black people think and what motivates them are the large subjects of the fiction written by Charles W. Chesnutt, the most acclaimed of turn-of-the-twentieth-century black fiction writers. Chesnutt was a shrewd observer of some features of black culture and a cool, dispassionate analyst of the national prejudice against blacks as well as reform strategies and programs. His short story collections, particularly *The Conjure Woman* (1889), had a large audience. His 1889 essay "What Is a White Man?" contained a sharp, detailed analysis of southern state laws (Chesnutt was a lawyer as well as a writer), defining how much black blood, or how absurdly little, it took to make a person legally black and other laws regulating "the intercourse of the races in schools and in the marriage relation."[13] His 1900 review of Booker T. Washington's *The Future of the American Negro*, on the other hand, laid out not just a picture of black social conditions and of Washington's program for improving "ignorant and untrained" people by teaching them skilled trades that could be marketed for good wages but also stated clearly how the whole country would be changed: "The American people are justly proud of their growing strength and prestige; they cannot devote them to a better use than to go manfully to work and get rid of this black nightmare that threatens the welfare and happiness of the whole country."[14] His 1901 novel, *The Marrow of Tradition*, is one of the era's fullest portrayals of black–white racial dynamics. It takes place against the backdrop of the 1898 Wilmington, NC, riot and involves some astute analysis of white fears of black political power.

Chesnutt's first story, "The Goophered Grapevine," published in August, 1887 in *The Atlantic*, was the first fiction by a black writer to appear in a major national magazine. Casual readers probably understood it to be an entertaining story about pre-War plantation life. Its main character, Uncle Julius, may have reminded them of Harris's Uncle Remus. It contained funny black dialect such as could be found in *Huckleberry Finn* and in the conventional stage comedy of the day. It involved black superstitions and had lots of descriptions of life in a fairly remote region of the South, thus

[13]   Charles W. Chesnutt, "What Is a White Man?" at http://www.online-literature.com/charles-chesnutt/wife-of-his-youth/10/

[14]   Charles W. Chesnutt, "Review of Booker T. Washington's *The Future of the American Negro*," at http://faculty.berea.edu/browners/chesnutt/Works/ReviewsbyChesnutt/plea.html

meeting the interests of the magazine audience in reading about other parts of the country.

"The Goophered Grapevine" also played to the interest of American farmers and others in grape production and consumption. The 1880s were sometimes described by contemporaries as a period of "grape fever." Articles on grape production appeared continually in newspapers and magazines like *The Independent*.[15] Grapes were associated with healthy living by "fruitarians" and vegetarians. One writer, quoted in Thomas Pinney's *A History of Wine in America* (1989), remarked that in the 1880s "Lawyers, teachers, doctors, and even ministers of the gospel turned vine-yardists." The sugar-packed scuppernong grape, native to North Carolina, which is the subject of the action of Chesnutt's story, became especially prominent during the period because it was the foundation grape for the renowned vintner and businessman Paul Garrett's "Virginia Dare" wine, for many decades the country's most popular. That the story's use of grapes appealed to audiences is evident in the fact that, just as it came out in the *Atlantic*, it was also published in the "Ladies Department" of the *Massachusetts Ploughman and New England Journal of Agriculture,* one of the country's most widely distributed agricultural newspapers.

Whatever his clever use of "grape fever" of the day as a vehicle, "The Goophered Grapevine" was about larger issues, grappling briefly but deftly with questions regarding the nature of rural southern black culture and challenging conventional contemporary beliefs about black–white rela-tionships. It remarked on the commonplace mixing of black and white "bloodlines" in the South, quickly disposing of notions of white purity. It explored black folk beliefs and their social utility, and it suggested that whites adopted black folk beliefs. It explored a fundamental motive among poor southern blacks, the constant search for decent food. It explored the fundamental motives of white people, the motive of the slave-owner in becoming a Confederate officer, and the motives of the white narrator.

In "What Is a White Man?" the essay he published two years later, Chesnutt wrote that "more than half of the colored people of the United States are of mixed blood." In "The Goophered Grapevine," the fact that people were "of all shades of complexion" was noted by the white northern narrator as the primary general feature of the residents of Patesville, North Carolina. One of the things he initially observed about Uncle Julius was

[15]   See, for instance, the issue of March 31, 1887 on "Fruit Eating" and of March 31, 1887 on "Grape Lore."

that he "was not entirely black" and that "There was a shrewdness in his eyes, too, which was not altogether African."[16] White and black mixing extended to matters of belief, too. Late in the story, Uncle Julius says matter-of-factly, with no surprise whatever, that it was Dugal' McAdoo, the slave-owner himself, who arranged for his vineyard to be conjured.

Within his conjure story, Uncle Julius provides very clear statements about his understanding of the fundamental motivations of white men. Dugal' McAdoo is motivated purely by money. He makes a thousand gallons of scuppernong wine a year, desires to make more, and pays the conjure woman to create a spell that will kill people who steal a handful of grapes. He makes a thousand dollars a year for several years by selling a vigorous but bewitched slave Henry to other men and repurchasing him when, like a grapevine, he annually withers away. He is so crazed about money that he becomes "bewitch" by a fake northern agricultural expert who promises to fix his vines to produce greater quantities of grapes. This northerner, the other white man spoken about in some detail by Uncle Julius, abuses McAdoo's hospitality by taking him for a thousand dollars at cards and then, hired by the feckless McAdoo to improve the vineyard, destroys it entirely by digging under the roots of the vine, pruning too severely, and applying the wrong fertilizer and sweetener. In short, McAdoo represents in Uncle Julius's story not a genteel plantation owner promoting a southern way of life but a cheating money-grubber. Later, when the Civil War began, McAdoo became an officer, motivated not by a desire to defend the southern way of life but by a desire "ter kill a Yankee fer eve'y dollar he los' 'long er dat grape-raisin' Yankee."

Black people in "The Goophered Grapevine" also cheat and steal. But they are motivated by their desire for food such as opossum, chicken, watermelon, and, when they are ripe, scuppernong grapes. Uncle Julius described the effect of the ripe grapes: the "scuppernon' make you smack yo' lip en roll yo' eye and wush fer mo'; so I reckon it ain't very 'stonishin' dat niggers lub scuppernon'." That language seems to be drawn from conventional racist descriptions of slobbering blacks. But, whatever its source, it accurately describes the degree to which slaves and free black poor people, too, were driven by the idea of consuming high protein food like opossum and chicken and food high in sugar content like watermelons and scuppernong grapes. The same quest – need, really – to acquire good

---

[16]   Charles Chesnutt, "The Goophered Grapevine," *Massachusetts Ploughman and New England Journal of Agriculture*, 46 (July 30, 1887), p. 4.

food can be found in a great many of the African-American folk tales later collected by folklorists. It is also manifested, it should be added, in a great number of white literary texts that focus on the desires of poor white people (hunger is not racially based; the need for protein and sugar is transcultural).

Uncle Julius did not comment on the motivations of the white narrator of the story's frame but, indirectly, Chesnutt did. The narrator speaks a fussy, high-toned dialect that suggests he is educated. He is rational and temperate. He is a man of taste, with a sense of the picturesque and an interest in architectural and horticultural ruins. He is wealthy, able to consider relocation to Spain or Italy to grow grapes while ministering to his sick wife, able to purchase an extensive former plantation, and able to live comfortably before his restoration of the vineyard yields some earnings (in grape production, it is usually six or seven years before there is a profitable yield). He probably does not need to work, for his description of himself as liking the business of grape culture and having "given it much study" makes him sound more like a gentleman farmer than a person who needs to farm to make money. At the end of the story, he makes himself sound benevolent when he describes how he suspects that his "colored assistants" (that is, his farm laborers) steal grapes, or, as he puts it more delicately, how they "do not suffer from the want of grapes during the season" and, also, how he has given Uncle Julius a job as a coachman as well as a cabin on the farm. Much of this makes the white narrator seem pompous and self-congratulatory.

But despite his obvious flaws, the narrator is nonetheless an entrepreneur who brings much-needed capital into the rural South, takes risks, creates jobs, and does decently for himself and for his adopted community. That is to say, "The Goophered Grapevine" ultimately provides not just an alternative understanding of a slave-owner's motivations, the motivations of blacks, and racial mixing but an alternative image of the northerner who came to the South during Reconstruction. In the standard southern story of Reconstruction, that northerner was a "carpetbagger," a fast-money artist interested only in himself. In Chesnutt's story, the plantation owner is the fast-money artist while the northern entrepreneur is honorable and observant and humane. As brief a story as it was, then, "The Goophered Grapevine" thoroughly and brilliantly subverted the conventional thinking of its time about black Americans and about Reconstruction.

3

Immigrants

The Context

Under the traditional "Open Door" immigration policy that prevailed in the United States, earlier nineteenth-century immigrants were mainly Protestants who came from northwestern European countries such as England and Germany. With rare exceptions, they were judged to be capable of assimilating to American life. In the 1840s, as a result of the Potato Famine in their home country, great numbers of Irish Catholics began to migrate to the US. Large-scale Irish immigration continued into the early twentieth century

Irish Catholics were for many decades perceived by "native" Americans – in the language of the day, a "native" was a white Protestant who had been in the country for a generation or so – as alien and unassimilable because they were superstitious, ignorant, subversive, and violent. The religious elements of this stereotype were rooted in centuries-old Protestant depictions of Roman Catholicism. The other elements were allegedly based on cool, reasoned observations of Irish Catholic behavior. Similar allegations, with concomitant stereotypes, were made against many later immigrant groups including the Chinese, Jews, and Italians. The formal result of an allegation about a particular group's unassimilable nature was the claim that immigration by members of that group needed to be slowed down or entirely stopped. The informal result was that those already in the country were marginalized, made to feel unwelcome, and worse.

Lots of jokes and stories about dumb Irishmen circulated. Newspaper advertisements for employment sometimes included the line that "No Irishmen Need Apply." More prominently, there were frequent newspaper reports in New York, Boston, and Philadelphia, the three gateway cities where large numbers settled, of Irish Catholic mob violence. Some of this violence was directed against black men with whom they competed for low-level laboring jobs. Much more was directed against white Protestants. Irish Catholics, on the other hand, were sometimes on the receiving end of violence mounted by organized "Nativist" political parties, which saw them as agents of the Pope (who had allegedly sent them to the US to subvert American institutions and the American way of life).

Enmity toward Irish Catholics increased substantially as a result of the three-day New York City Draft Riot (that is, the riot against conscription into the Union army) that began on July 13, 1863. July 13 was less than two weeks after the end of the Battle of Gettysburg and that must have convinced many northern observers that Irish Catholics were grotesquely anti-Union. Standard newspaper stories about the riot usually stressed the burning of the Colored Orphan Asylum as a particularly egregious example of Irish Catholic monstrousness against innocent victims, the burning of the Second Avenue militia Armory as a clear instance of subversion, and the attack on the offices of the *New York Tribune* as a dramatic demonstration of disrespect for the free press, a core American institution. Decades later, the Draft Riot was still being recalled. For example, *King's Handbook of New York City*, a 900-page guide to the city published in 1892, remembered that:

> The closed shops, the streets clear of their customary traffic, and even of omnibuses and horse-cars, and many of the houses prepared like fortresses for defense, gave the city a singular and ominous appearance, which was increased by the mad roars of the mob, the clattering of cavalry along the pavement, the roll of volley-firing, and the heavy booming of artillery, sweeping the riotous vermin from the streets.[1]

More than a thousand people were killed and wounded, according to *King's*, and two million dollars worth of property was destroyed.

One of the main themes in the 50 or more years of extreme anti-Irish Catholic agitation in the US was their alleged inability to leave behind their antagonisms against other national groups when they migrated to the US. What was seen as a spectacular illustration of this inability occurred in 1866, when some 10,000 Union and Confederate Irish-Catholic veterans became the so-called American wing of the Irish Revolutionary Brotherhood,

---

[1]   *King's Handbook of New York City: An Outline History and Description of the American Metropolis* (Moses King, Boston, 1892), p. 42.

under the command of former Union General Thomas Sweeney. The plan of the Brotherhood was to strike a blow against the hated British Empire by invading Canada and helping Irish-Catholic Canadians form a new republic. There was an actual invasion into Canada near Buffalo, NY, by a column of 1,200 men, which was immediately and easily defeated by the British regular army and Canadian militias.

Less spectacular but perhaps more symptomatic of the Old World baggage that the Irish allegedly carried into the US were the interethnic riots frequently reported in the press. A March 1868 article that appeared in the respectable *Round Table* provided unusually full details about conventional perceptions of the causes and effects of interethnic tensions. It began by noting that, because New York business was stagnant and there was no work available, immigration authorities had moved some recent arrivals from Germany and Ireland to Ward's Island in the harbor. There was soon trouble:

A German was carrying a cup of water and an Irishman in sport upset it. The two had a dispute, ending in a fight, during which the Irishman was stabbed by his opponent. On the following day a group of about three hundred Germans made an attack on some Irish people in the washhouse and drove them away. The latter immediately aroused all their compatriots in the neighborhood who, in considerable force, broke open a tool-house and took thence pitchforks, scythes, axes, and everything else that might be used as a weapon, even, it is said, breaking up mowing machines to get the knives. Thus provided, they marched with a green flag to attack the Germans, who had repaired to the basement of the hospital building and barricaded the doors. The Irish, however, made a violent rush upon these defenses and forced their way into the building. A terrible battle ensued, in which, it is said, the Germans were getting much the worst of it, the prospect being that they would all be killed. ... The crowd was so great as to prevent the police from entering the hall ... and, as the only means of saving the Germans, the superintendent took the responsibility of ordering the police to fire into the crowd. ... Eighty prisoners were taken, and some thirty of the rioters were found to be wounded.[2]

The story contained a number of lessons for its readers, and in that regard it summarized many of the standard concerns about immigrants in

---

[2] "Race Hatred and the Suffrage," *The Round Table: A Saturday Review of Politics, Finance. Literature, Society*, March 14, 1868, p. 164.

general and Irish Catholics in particular. It indicated that such people could be provoked to violence by a trivial incident, that the situation could spin out of control in a flash, that the rioters were very resourceful in terms of procuring weapons, that they rapidly formed into murderous battle groups based solely on national origin, and that the police could not cope without resorting to deadly force. Later in the article, the author remarked with astonishment that such people would soon vote in American elections and that someday some of them would become the country's leaders. He dismissed the idea that they could be educated, given that they would have to spend most of their waking hours working under brutalizing conditions. He ended by calling for public discussion of whether the country should follow the received "democratic dogmas" about open immigration.

In the 1870s, a number of riots pitting Irish Catholics against Irish Protestants were reported in the press. The so-called "Orange Riot" of 1871 began with a New York parade marking a major event in their history by Protestant Irishmen. Anticipating trouble, officials ordered a militia regiment to accompany the parade. A shot was fired at the militia by one of the Irish Catholic hecklers who lined the parade route. The militia fired back and a gun battle ensued. Within a few minutes, two militiamen were killed, 24 militiamen and police were wounded, 31 Irish Catholics were killed, and another 67 were wounded.[3] Other riots reported in the press were smaller but still fearsome. One in the small textile manufacturing city of Lawrence, Massachusetts, for example, seems not to have killed anyone, only to have injured a dozen or so Protestants, but did major property damage, according to a July 1875 account in the *New York Observer and Chronicle*.[4] Some riots were presented as cautionary stories. An example of such a story was an August 1878 article in the *Observer and Chronicle* that told how Irish Catholic rioters had recently terrorized the Canadian city of Ottawa, and New Yorkers were told to learn the lesson that "an ounce of prevention is worth a pound of cure." The writer summarized recent history in colorful language calculated to inflame the passions of his readers:

> We have seen this city in the hands of Roman Catholic rioters: we have seen innocent men shot down, others hung at lamp posts, houses burned, and women and children flying from them in terror, and all this and more

---

[3] The 1871 Orange riot was best described and given context in the 5,000-word article "Noted Riots in New York; 1712 to 1871," *New York Times*, July 29, 1877, p. 10.

[4] "Roman Catholic Riots," *New York Observer and Chronicle*, July 15, 1875, p. 222.

the doings of infuriated Roman Catholics, insanely seeking to rule the city and to put down classes and individuals obnoxious to them.

The writer thought that conflicts with Roman Catholics would continue because, he said, "It is impossible to get into the head of an ignorant, whiskey-drinking foreigner, that in a land of liberty, law is to govern all classes alike."[5]

In the first half of the 1870s, newspaper reports about Irish Catholics displaying their ignorance and violence in city riots were complemented by reports of the violence in the Pennsylvania coal fields perpetrated by members of the Irish "Ancient Order of Hibernians," the "Molly McGuires," against employers. The agitation against the "Mollies" crested in early 1877 with the hanging of several of them in Pottsville, Pennsylvania. These events involving Irish Catholics were in the same time frame, readers will remember, as the fierce, widespread antiblack riots in the South during Reconstruction. The hangings in Pottsville were also a few months before the widespread Railroad Strikes of the summer 1877 that were sometimes referred to as a near-insurrection by American workers. Ironically, all of these violent, near-cataclysmic events of the 1870s took place while the nation was preparing for and celebrating its 100th anniversary and the era's technological, business, and other accomplishments in the great Centennial Exposition in Philadelphia. The events outlined above demonstrate the era's characteristic violence and, simultaneously, as in the case of the Centennial, its occasional expressions of national harmony and progress.

In any case, despite all the reports of their unassimilable nature and despite all the agitation against them, there were by the 1880s, 40 years after the beginning of their mass immigration, some clear indications that Irish Catholics were in fact assimilating or, at least, accommodating themselves to American society. While some newspapers portrayed them as only living in festering tenements in a few large cities, Irish Catholics had by then settled in every state, in most cities large and small, in the farmlands, and in small towns. They moved into virtually every unskilled, skilled, and commercial occupation. In New York, Boston, Philadelphia, Chicago, and, to a lesser but still significant extent, in San Francisco, they moved successfully into politics, mostly as Democrats, and by the 1890s they controlled a number of big city political machines. That translated into stable jobs for Irish Catholics in the construction and transportation industries and in

---

[5] "Religious Riots," *New York Observer and Chronicle*, August 22, 1878, p. 266.

municipal sanitation, police, and fire departments, as well as access to the great array of business and commercial opportunities that political control enabled. This is not to say that resistance to Irish Catholics crumbled because of their success. It did not. Individual Irishmen were still stereotyped as dumb, hard-drinking, brawling, and profane; the phrase "Irish politician" was often used as a synonym for "corrupt"; and the more extreme nativists continued to depict them as alien agents of the Pope. But their success, and their numbers, gave Irish Catholics the power to cope with such resistance.

Agitation against Irish Catholics reached one of its crests in the 1870s. So, too, did agitation against Chinese immigrants, though much of that agitation was restricted to the state of California, where they were most numerous. Popular white outcries about the Chinese focused on allegations about their unassimilable natures, their clannishness, their peculiar diets, their uncleanliness, their bestial lust for white women, and their willingness to work for low pay and thereby depress the wages of white men. Anti-Chinese riots occurred in many Pacific coast towns. Calls to stop the Chinese from entering the country, led by Pacific coast legislators, were loud, emotional, and utterly at odds with their extremely small numbers. Perhaps owing precisely to those small numbers, as well as to the fact that they were a *racial* group similar to blacks, the agitation to exclude them worked. In 1882, Congress passed the Chinese Exclusion Act, denying admission to Chinese laborers for the next 10 years. Any Chinese who used his or her hands while working was defined as a "laborer," so in effect the Act also prohibited immigration by doctors, engineers, merchants, and other skilled workers as well as immigration by manual laborers. Later, the Exclusion Act was extended indefinitely.

Between 1800 and 1880, more than 10 million immigrants entered the United States. Immigration significantly increased in the 1880s, then accelerated between 1891 and 1914, when more than 12 million immigrants arrived. Arrivals in the peak year of 1907 included 338,000 people from Austria-Hungary, with large numbers of Jews among them, 286,000 Italians, and 259,000 mostly Jewish Russians. For the entire period from 1899 to 1924, 3.8 million Italians, 3.4 million Slavs, and 1.8 million Jews were admitted to the US. In terms of their cultural and religious practices, such people, like their Irish Catholic and Chinese predecessors, were seen as dramatically different. They, too, faced questions about whether they could adapt to American ways.

Of the new immigrants, Jews received the most attention. This was probably because of their concentration in New York, which made them easily accessible as a subject to the legion of journalists and other writers who worked in the City's booming print media industry. But it was also because of their success as a group. In the 1890s and in the first decade of the new century, some of the mainstream newspaper and magazine commentary about Jews was quite positive regarding that success, sometimes seeing them as a kind of model immigrant group. An article called "The Jews of New York," which appeared in *Century* in January 1892, was typical, commenting extensively on Jewish business success in various kinds of manufacture and on the emerging Jewish dominance of wholesale trade, especially in the core Manhattan area from Canal Street to 14th Street (almost all of the 400 buildings on lower Broadway were said to be occupied by Jewish firms). The writer also reported that, judging by police reports, and contrary to popular opinion, Jews were less prone to fraud than Christians.[6] A September 1893 article in the Christian magazine *The Congregationalist* noted the rise of anti-Semitism in America, describing it as totally unfair treatment of immigrants who had been pushed out of Russia by persecution. The writer argued that recent Jewish immigrants had proven themselves to be model citizens, and he called on Christians to open their hearts and arms to Jews.[7] An April 1907 *New York Observer and Chronicle* article reported that New York City now had the largest concentration of Jews on earth and that "They are peaceable neighbors, they are good citizens, so far as enlightened. They take care of their own poor and helpless; they do not fill our jails and are seldom to be seen in our police courts." This article also remarked, hopefully, that Jews appeared to be open to the possibility of conversion to Christianity.[8]

But Jews were pictured by some elements of American society – who did not read or write balanced articles in tolerant mainstream periodicals – in much the same way that they had been pictured in Europe for hundreds of years. The allegations against them were, indeed, the standard trans-European allegations simply relocated to American soil: Jews had killed Christ; Jews controlled banking and thereby made it difficult for

---

[6]   Richard Wheatley, "The Jews of New York," *Century Illustrated Magazine*, 43 (January 1892), pp. 323–43.

[7]   "Anti-Semitism in America," *Congregationalist*, September 14, 1893, p. 78.

[8]   "Increase of Jews in America," *New York Observer and Chronicle*, April 4, 1907, p. 444.

Christians to do business; Jews were miserly; Jews kidnapped Christian children, murdered them, and drank their blood; and Jews (just like blacks and Chinese!) lusted for white American women. To these charges, as we will see, a number of other charges were added in later years regarding the propensity of Jews to be political agitators, subversives, sympathizers with black Americans, and Communists.

Italians also received considerable attention, much of it negative. In 1904, William D. Foulke, a US Civil Service Commissioner, provided readers of *Outlook* magazine with a summary of the unfortunate general beliefs about Italian immigrants:

> We fancy them ignorant, priest-ridden, lazy, unclean, dishonest, and revengeful. They have ways that we do not like. For instance, in their quarrels they use the knife rather than the nobler pistol which they cannot afford to buy. We picture the land they come from as the home of the brigand, the Anarchist, and the Mafia, and we fear that they will corrupt our citizenship and taint out blood.[9]

Foulke himself actually thought that Italians and other immigrants were bringing "vigor" to the country. But there were during this period great numbers of less tolerant commentators, many of whom seemed taken aback by what they saw as the physical disabilities of Italians, including their shortness and their untrustworthy eyes. In May 1910, *McClure's Magazine* published a "scientific" article in this vein. Burton J. Hendrick's illustrated article reported on how the author's measurements of the heads of living subjects proved that in the New York City environment "short-headed" Jews were becoming "long-headed," which was a very good thing for Jewish sociability and intelligence, but "long-headed" Sicilians were, unfortunately, becoming "short-headed."[10]

Discussion of Italian criminality began shortly after 1900. In May 1909, the beginning of organized Italian crime was reported extensively in *McClure's*. In an article about the "Black Hand" gangsters, Arthur Woods wrote of how some criminal Italian "parasites" were practicing extortion, commercial swindling, and the like, and argued that the problem was becoming so severe that the country needed to develop a "secret police

[9] William D. Foulke, "A Word on Italian Immigration," *Outlook*, 74 (February 20, 1904), pp. 459–61.
[10] Burton J. Hendrick, "The Skulls of Our Immigrants," *McClure's Magazine*, 35 (May 1910), pp. 36–52.

system" to keep the Black Handers under surveillance.[11] This was one of the earliest of many such discussions.

The vast majority of Italian immigrants of the era were young male "birds of passage." That is, they were temporary immigrants who came to the US to earn money, developed few ties or loyalties, and returned to their native villages and cities, in the best-case scenarios, with their pockets filled with cash. Their rates of return to Italy, as sometimes reported by government agencies, were startling. In April 1912, for instance, *Outlook* magazine reported that immigration authorities had recently noted that 222,235 Italian laborers had entered the country in 1910 and that the number who went back to Italy that year was 92,947; and that 155,835 laborers had come in 1911 but that 139,364 had left. Net immigration was, then, 129,288 in 1910 and 16,190 in 1911. Such reports on "birds of passage" might be expected to have allayed the fears of Nativists and others that Italian immigrants were swamping the US and might soon change it to a nation of hot-headed, dwarfish gangsters. In standard accounts, however, the reports did not allay fears but, as in the *Outlook* article, served as an argument for a new national immigration policy that would only admit people "who come to make permanent homes for themselves."[12]

Politicians and commentators in the mainstream press assumed that all right-thinking, ambitious people desperately wanted to become permanent residents of the US, the "greatest country the world has ever known," in the popular phrase. But the return migration, that is, the return to their home countries of immigrants of many origins, not just Italians, was some-times noticed. In November 1910, the *New York Times* reported that about 400,000 immigrants returned to their homes each year.[13] In September 1913, the *Times*, which had noted over the years that immigrants were sending millions of dollars annually back to Europe, announced in a some-what bitter headline that "Immigrants [were] Rehabilitating Europe With Our Money."[14] "Our money" here meant money that had been earned in the US. There was, however, so far as I know, no sustained investigation of the *causes* of return migration. It might have been possible that American

[11] Arthur Woods, "The Problem of the Black Hand," *McClure's Magazine*, 33 (May 1909), pp. 40–8.
[12] "Italian Immigration," *Outlook*, April 27, 1912, p. 883.
[13] "Important Immigrants: The 400,000 Who Return to Their Homes Each Year," *New York Times*, November 28, 1910, p. 8.
[14] "Immigrants Rehabilitating Europe With Our Money," *New York Times*, September 21, 1913, p. SM7.

life did not meet the aspirations of some immigrants, or that some immigrants longed for their old lives, or that they loved the countries of their birth, or that some immigrants came only to make money and left when they had enough, or that the coarse, pervasive anti-immigrant prejudice of significant numbers of Americans was too much to bear. But those ideas were not explored and the official and unofficial core narrative of America as the desired destiny of the world's multitudes continued unabated.

The resistance of some elements of American society to the presence of some new immigrants continued. Sometimes resistance involved entire communities. Because they were so close to New York and Philadelphia, and contained industrial centers like Newark and Paterson, early twentieth-century small New Jersey communities could reasonably be expected to have overcome fear and loathing about immigrants. Many did not, became hotbeds of anti-immigrant agitation, and prided themselves on being "racially" pure or nearly pure. Advertising their virtues in the 1911 *Industrial Directory of New Jersey*, attempting to get manufacturers to relocate to their towns, communities near Philadelphia, such as Moorestown, Mount Holly, and Lumberton, said that their populations of "foreign immigrants" was small, that "practically no foreign immigrants reside in the town." The ocean resort community of Cape May said it only contained some hundred Italian laborers, "employed on public improvements." Communities like Oradell and Waldwick, close to New York, Newark, and Paterson, advertised themselves in much the same way.

The attitudes of some Americans about immigrants was dramatically manifested in the Leo M. Frank case that unfolded in 1915. Frank, a Jewish, Brooklyn-reared, Cornell University engineering graduate whose wife came from a wealthy Atlanta, Georgia, family, was the superintendent of the National Pencil Factory in Atlanta. One of his employees, 13-year-old Mary Phagan, was raped and murdered at the factory, and Frank was accused.

He stood trial in an extremely charged atmosphere, with newspapers publishing wholly fabricated stories about Jewish sexual orgies at the factory and Frank's involvements with other Christian girls and women. His Jewish origins were emphasized and sensationalized. Without any clear evidence of his involvement and, according to some observers, with some evidence pointing clearly to a black janitor as the perpetrator, Frank was found guilty and sentenced to death. The case was appealed all the way to the US Supreme Court, which affirmed the conviction and sentence by a 7–2 margin (in his dissent, Justice Oliver Wendell Holmes captured the poisoned atmosphere surrounding Franks' trial when he commented that "Mob law does not become due process of law by securing the assent of a terrorized jury"). Ultimately, though, Frank's sentence to be hanged was commuted to life in prison by the governor of Georgia, John M. Slaton.

Outrage at Governor Slaton's action ensued. A group that included leading citizens such as a former governor of Georgia, a judge, lawyers, and the son of a US Senator, engineered Frank's removal from jail, according to the lengthy *New York Times* report of August 19, 1915.[15] He was transported 175 miles across four Georgia counties. He was then hanged in the woods outside Marietta, Mary Phagan's home town, in front of hundreds of eyewitnesses.

Some of the participants in the Frank lynching styled themselves "The Knights of Mary Phagan," using the word "Knight" in the manner in which the Ku Klux Klan had used it to describe its warriors during Reconstruction. This was, as it would turn out, prophetic, because on Thanksgiving night of 1915, three months after Leo Frank was lynched, a number of those Knights of Mary Phagan joined a local minister named William J. Simmons at Stone Mountain, Georgia, where they ignited a cross and thus symbolically founded a new, modern Ku Klux Klan. A couple of weeks later, on December 6, following the Atlanta showing of *The Birth of a Nation*, the white supremacist film commemorating the 50th anniversary of the end of the Civil War, Simmons, the Knights, and a number of other people paraded as the new Klan on Peachtree Avenue, Atlanta's great street. This was the first public performance by what would become in the 1920s a major, nationally based social movement which, like the predecessor Klan, was interested in maintaining the virtual enslavement of blacks but was even more profoundly interested in bringing back an earlier, purer, immigrant-free country that was, in the phrase of the day, "100% American."

The Literature

In an autobiographical essay titled "Choosing a Dream," Mario Puzo, born in 1920 in New York City to Italian parents and later famous as the author of *The Godfather*, said that his mother thought he had gone crazy when, at age 16, he announced that he was going to be a great writer. "She was illiterate," Puzo wrote, "and her peasant life in Italy made her believe that

---

[15] "Grim Tragedy in Woods," *New York Times*, August 19, 1915, p 1.

only a son of the nobility could possibly be a writer. Artistic beauty after all could spring only from the seedbed of fine clothes, fine food, luxurious living."[16] The peasant's life, whether in Italy or America, was about finding work, making a living, and caring for family. Puzo's comment is applicable to other immigrant groups, not just Italians. For the vast majority of immigrants, life was about struggling to live, not about art and self-expression. Many groups, like the Italians, did not begin to write about their immigrant experiences for decades.

No Irish-American literature reflecting on the immigrant experience was published until the early 1890s, when journalist Finley Peter Dunne began to write newspaper columns featuring the monologues of his character Mr. Dooley. In thick dialect, Mr. Dooley, a Chicago bartender, expressed Irish-American folkways, traditions, struggles, political and social beliefs, and successes. Over several hundred columns and several book collections, Dunne provided a very complete ethnography of Chicago Irish-American culture across generations. Mr. Dooley, incidentally, was often very wise about assimilation, as when he ironically recounted the "glorious rayciption" he got when he arrived in America: "Th' stars an' sthripes whispered a welcome in th' breeze an' a shovel was thrust into me hand an' I was pushed into a sthreet excyvatin' as though I'd been born here."

Irish-American culture and characters appeared in fiction written by major writers. Mark Twain conveyed something of the flavor of standard anti-Irish feeling in "Buck Fanshawe's Funeral," part of *Roughing It* (1872), when he used "No Irish Need Apply" as a refrain. Twain no doubt also meant his Pap Finn, Huck's father in *Huckleberry Finn* (1885), to be a portrait of the stereotypical drunken, profane, and ignorant Irishman (Finn is a common Irish surname). Many of Stephen Crane's low Bowery characters in *Maggie: A Girl of the Streets* (1893) are assimilated Irish; his Scully, in "The Blue Hotel," an Irishman who speaks with a modified brogue, presides over the whiskey-induced violence of that story. The complexities of small town Irish-American culture, including the high culture of the very successful Irish, were explored by Harold Frederic in *The Damnation of Theron Ware* (1897).

Turn-of-the-century jokes about Irishmen often emphasized their wild, profane sexuality. Irish girls were often pictured as highly sexual and

[16]   Mario Puzo, "Choosing a Dream: Italians in Hell's Kitchen," in Wesley Brown and Amy Ling (eds), *Visions of America: Personal Narratives from the Promised Land* (Persea Books, New York, 1993), pp. 48–59; quotation p. 50.

sensual. Celia Madden in *The Damnation of Theron Ware*, a devotee of art and beauty and the unconventional, was the temptress of the young minister Theron Ware, ushering him into a world his own conventional background did not prepare him to understand. The very young Aileen Butler, the beautiful daughter of a successful Irish politician in Theodore Dreiser's *The Financier*, became Frank Cowperwood's mistress and, later, his second wife. In Jack London's "South of the Slot," a young working-class woman who is not described as Irish but who has a commonplace Irish name, Mary Condon, is portrayed as vital, free, and passionate. One might be tempted to argue that the image of the hot Irish girl is just another reductive stereotype. But I think that, for the time, it represents a challenge to the conventional image of the Irish, an advance toward a fuller sense of their complex humanity. Especially in literature written by men, the sexualization of immigrant women represents a kind of progress.

At the turn of the twentieth century and for many years afterward, Jews were the most widely discussed immigrants because as non-Christians they were the most alien and threatening and because of their great numbers on the Lower East Side of Manhattan, said to be the most densely populated area in the world. They astonished countless observers, including cosmopolitan men like the writer Henry James. James left the United States in 1875 to live permanently in England, returning for visits in 1883 and 1904. The latter visit produced *The American Scene* (1907), where he recorded his impressions of various parts of the country. Much had changed over the years but no changes were more extreme than those he noted in Manhattan, where he described himself as "haunted" by his "sense of dispossession." Riding on a streetcar, he remarked that he only saw foreigners, "a row of faces, up and down, testifying, without exception, to alienism unmistakable, alienism undisguised and unashamed." After seeing the Lower East Side, he spoke of the "Hebrew conquest of New York." Unlike so many harsher, meaner, more threatened commentators, James did not descend into hysteria because of the "alienism." Rather, he finally described himself as "agreeably baffled" by "Remarkable, unspeakable New York!"

Jewish writers were the most articulate about the immigrant experience, primarily because so many arrived in America with a high degree of literacy, understood the power gained by quickly learning English, and had a more democratic understanding than other groups of who was entitled to be a writer. Very early fictions like Abraham Cahan's *Yekl: A Tale of the New York Ghetto* (1896) and *The Imported Bridegroom and Other Stories* (1898) provided readers with some understanding of the oppressions Jews had suffered in Russia, the difficulties of emigration, the texture of

Jewish-American daily life, the tensions that existed among and between Jews, and the issues involved in assimilation. *Yekl* was especially sharp in portraying how rapidly some Jews adapted, often imperfectly, to American ways and how quickly they came to be repulsed by old world customs. "The Imported Bridegroom," the title story of the 1898 collection, was encyclopedic about the contrasts between old world and new world Jewish cultures. Cahan's later *The Rise of David Levinsky* (1917) was the most complete of the early twentieth-century fictional accounts of assimilation. The novel also contained extraordinarily sharp portrayals of dissident Jewish socialist subcultures, the garment industry in which Jews achieved great prominence, and upper-middle-class Jewish consumer culture. In Cahan's fiction, Jews were portrayed as complex people and Jewish-American culture was pictured as multidimensional, full of class antagonisms, and given to rapid change because of the pressures of the modern new world of America.

The conflict between parents and children over traditions and assimilation was a prime subject of Jewish-American fiction. Anzia Yezierska, who emerged as a prominent writer in the years after World War I, used intergenerational conflict as one of her major themes. Her "The Fat of the Land," named the best of *The Best Short Stories of 1919*, told of the hard times of a poor New York Jewish family and how the children of that family achieve lives of comfort. The children take care of their mother, moving her out of her impoverished neighborhood, but they are ashamed of her because of her vulgar peasant ways. A daughter considers her mother to be a "black shadow" of her past, telling her brother, "I've borne the shame of mother while you bought her off with a present and a treat here and there. God knows how hard I tried to civilize her so as not to have to blush with shame whenever I take her anywhere."

The mother in the story, however, is presented as not deserving better treatment because she subjected her children to interminable screaming and abuse. Calling one child a "bloodsucker," she complained, "Could anybody keep that brat clean? I wash him one minute, and he is dirty the minute after." On another occasion, she complained, "Mine life is so black for my eyes! Some mothers got luck. A child gets run over by a car, some fall from a window, some burn themselves up with a match, some get choked with diphtheria; but no death takes mine away." There is a great body of writing about immigrants which exalts family relations, the self-sacrificing of parents and the thankfulness of children. In "The Fat of the Land," in her 1920 short story "The Lost 'Beautifulness,'" and in her

Bread Givers (1925), Yezierska refused to subscribe to those conventional pieties.

Yezierska was also one of the earliest immigrant writers to reject the idea that immigrants should be grateful to America. In "The Lost 'Beautifulness,'" she questioned what America gave back to immigrants whose sons fought in World War I. In "America and I," an autobiographical essay published in *Children of Loneliness* (1923), she spoke passionately about the desire of Jews to assimilate and to contribute to American society and about the resistance of America to Jews: "Between my soul and the American soul were worlds of difference that no words could bridge over."

In response to their most vociferous critics, who argued that they were incurably alien and should therefore be excluded from the country, some Jews made counterarguments that they were endlessly grateful to America and wanted above all to become good Americans. The most famous statement of these arguments was in Mary Antin's *The Promised Land* (1912). For Antin, who emigrated with her family in 1894 but later completely shed her Jewishness, America was the "golden hope" of the world. *The Promised Land* was duly appreciated by reviewers and Antin was celebrated as a model immigrant: her essay "A Woman to her Fellow-Citizens" was featured in *Outlook* in November 1912 and, according to the *New York Times* in February 1913, she was one of the featured speakers at a Lincoln Day dinner for 2,500 people at which the Progressive Party candidacy of Theodore Roosevelt for President was announced.[17]

Large, complicated questions such as whether America was a land of opportunity or not, whether America welcomed its immigrants or not, and whether America immigrants were treated humanely and as equals were widely discussed, often by important writers. Two of the most important early twentieth-century novels that focus on the experience of immigrant characters, and come to astonishingly different conclusions about the large questions, are Upton Sinclair's *The Jungle* (1906) and Willa Cather's *O Pioneers!* (1913). In a later chapter, I shall discuss *The Jungle* in some detail. For the present, I will say only that it argues that immigrants have no chance for real success. Cather's novel, on the other hand, argues the position that the country gives a great deal to immigrants, or at least to those who have proper outlooks.

---

[17] Mary Antin, "A Woman to her Fellow Citizens," *Outlook*, November 2, 1912, pp. 482–6; "Roosevelt Named as 1916 Candidate," *New York Times*, February 13, 1913, p. 5.

O Pioneers! takes place from the late 1870s to the late 1890s in southern Nebraska. Its immigrant characters – Norwegians, Swedes, Bohemians, and French – are homesteaders, people who came into possession of their land through the Homestead Act of 1862. Many had never farmed before but had been attracted to farming because homesteaders received 160 acres of publicly owned land for free if they lived on it for five years. They faced brutally hard work, of course. They also faced the challenges of farming, including crop failures and extended droughts. Cather knew about these challenges. She lived in Red Cloud in southern Nebraska from the time she was 10, when her family moved there from Virginia, until she graduated from the University of Nebraska in 1895. During her college years, Nebraska farmers were hit as hard as farmers anywhere by the depression that followed the 1893 Panic. They then suffered from a severe drought in 1894. Throughout 1895, the destitution of many Nebraska farmers was widely reported in the national press.[18]

In "The Wild Land," the first section of *O Pioneers!*, Cather broadly sketched out the primitive living conditions the homesteaders endured, the harsh weather, their endless work, their slender profits during the first 20 years of settlement. Some homesteaders left during hard times, heading off to cities. Others persisted, and by the 1890s, when much of the novel is set, the land has been profoundly changed, in Cather's imagination if not in fact. Now, Cather wrote, its "rich soil yields heavy harvests; the dry, bracing climate and the smoothness of the land make labor easy for men and for beasts." When plowed, the land "rolls away" from the steel blade "with a soft, deep sigh of happiness." At harvest time, the wheat grain "is so heavy that it bends toward the blade and cuts like velvet."

Immigrants prosper as a result of the soil's power. Telephone wires testify to their access to modern conveniences. From the graveyard where some of the original settlers lie buried, "one can count a dozen gaily painted farmhouses; the gilded weather-vanes on the big red barns wink at each other across the green and brown and yellow fields."

Alexandra Bergson, the heroic Norwegian immigrant woman who stands at the center of this prosperity, was raised in a sod house but now

---

[18] For example, "Suffering in Nebraska: Actual Destitution Reported in Many of the Counties," *New York Times*, January 2, 1895, p. 11; "Nebraska's Destitution: Intense Suffering of the Starving, Half-Clothed People," *New York Times*, February 17, 1895, p. 5; "Their Pitiable Plight: People in Nebraska Had No Other Resources When Crops Failed," *New York Times*, February 22, 1895, p. 14.

lives in a "big white house" surrounded by many sheds and outbuildings. The description of Alexandra's property could have been written by a real estate developer with a good knowledge of the devices used by landscape architects. The mile-long road leading to the house was lined on both sides by "tall osage orange hedges, their glossy green marking off the yellow fields" while nearby there was an orchard "knee-deep in timothy grass" surrounded by a mulberry hedge. "Order and fine arrangement," we are told, is manifested everywhere on the great farm, "in the windbreaks and sheds, in the symmetrical pasture ponds, planted with scrub willows to give shade to the cattle in fly-time. There is even a white row of beehives in the orchard, under the walnut trees. You feel that, properly, Alexandra's house is the big out-of-doors, and that it is in the soil that she expressed herself best."

Cather described Alexandra as wholesome, healthy, and clean. In many scenes, she was associated with the colors white, gold, and red. She has "faith," a deep sense of tradition, a respect for her elders, a love of reading, a "slow, truthful, and steadfast mind," and an active imagination. Other immigrants in *O Pioneers!* are decent, God-fearing, wholesome, and community-minded. Rather than hostilities between groups, there is mixing and friendship across ethnic lines; French people, Norwegians, Bohemians, and Swedes even intermarry and occasionally worship together. The Norwegian Alexandra employs Swedish girls as domestics and an Irishman as her manager. All of this amounted to as optimistic a view of immigrant destinies as any written in the era.

How was the grim, unyielding land faced by the original homesteaders transformed; how did prosperity and community success come about? Two reviews of *O Pioneers!* anticipated the responses of later readers. An unsigned review published in the *Bookman* described the novel as "a study of the struggles and privations of the foreign emigrant in the Herculean task of subduing the untamed prairie land of the Far West and making it yield something more than a starvation income."[19] This suggested that the transformation was the result of the persistent hard work of the homesteaders. It did not seem to recognize that many of the homesteaders in the novel, beaten down by the unyielding land, gave up and moved on. Another unsigned review, published in *McClure's Magazine* (where, incidentally, Cather worked as an editor from 1906 to 1912), stressed the role of Alexandra Bergson in bringing about the change. The reviewer described

---

[19] "O Pioneers," *Bookman*, 37 (August 1913), p. 666.

Alexandra as "a sort of Nebraska Valkyr, with the daring and confidence of one who carries a new message. The forces of the New World have freed her from the old tradition of woman as a dependent drudge, pouring out her life in self-sacrifice and submission."[20] This suggested that the transformation derived not so much from hard work but from Alexandra's vision, which many later readers defined as epic and mythic. Many textual details – references to the Bible, to creation and fertility myths, to epic and pastoral literary traditions – support this understanding of Alexandra.

In traditional literary terms, Alexandra is indeed an epic figure and a fertility goddess whose "faith" in and love of the land poetically transformed it and, consequently, transformed the lives of the homesteaders who stuck it out. She is also, obviously, a woman, and in that regard she represents the large contemporary idea that women can be the equals of men and that some men – in her case, her father – recognized women's potential and gave them the chance. But Alexandra is a particular kind of epic hero, fertility goddess, and female leader. She is a hero, a goddess, and a leader who possesses a sound business plan, a creative business vision for material success. At the end of the first part of the novel, "The Wild Land," Alexandra, during hard times when lots of people were giving up and leaving, announces her business vision to her conventional, conformist, unimaginative brothers, telling them about her plan to borrow money and to buy up neighbors' land (eventually, the family will have 1,400 acres). Alexandra's goal is for her family to become in 10 years "independent landowners, not struggling farmers any longer," not overworked, old-fashioned laborers on the land but smart investors and managers. Her goal involves her businesswoman's faith that the land will appreciate in value, making them rich. But it also involves practical, scientific farm management, as when she tells her brothers that they should raise the new kind of clover and, later, that "alfalfa has been the salvation of this country," recounts how they resisted when she began planting wheat instead of corn, and how she built the first grain storage silo in the region. In addition, Alexandra is shown to be a model employer, looking out for the welfare of her employees and even eating with them.

One of the great debates of the era, as of any American era, was about who creates wealth. The American business press and much of the mainstream press argued that business people were the wealth creators. They had ideas that conventional people might resist, they accepted risk, tested

---

[20] "O Pioneers!" *McClure's Magazine*, 41 (July 1913), p. 199.

their idea, and in many cases the idea proved itself, giving them wealth while building community prosperity. *O Pioneers!* traces exactly that pattern in the career of Alexandra. The other answer to the question of who creates wealth was the ordinary people, the workers. This was the answer of dissident political movements such as the Populist movement of the 1890s, socialist movements, and labor unions. In *O Pioneers!* this answer is embodied in Alexandra's dullard brothers, Oscar and Lou, and in the character of Frank Shabata, who murders his wife, Marie, and her lover, Alexandra's youngest brother, Emil. Including Marie, these are all people who act out of unrestrained passion.

Cather carefully described the radical politics of Oscar, Lou, and Frank. Like a worker resistant to workplace changes, to efficiencies, Oscar "felt there was a sovereign virtue in mere bodily toil, and he rather liked to do things in the hardest way." Both he and Lou would have been content with having a "steady job, a few holidays, [and] nothing to think about." Lou becomes a politician, about which Cather says, "Politics being the natural field for such talents, he neglects his farm to attend conventions and to run for county office." Lou is a Populist, blustering on about 1896 Presidential candidate William Jennings Bryan and about the unfairness with which the East has mistreated the West. Frank Shabata, on the other hand, is pictured as handsome, self-absorbed, agitated, and envious of others. Cather says that "Frank was always reading about the doings of rich people and feeling outraged. He had an inexhaustible stock of stories about their crimes and follies, how they bribed the courts and shot down their butlers with impunity whenever they chose. Frank and Lou Bergson had very similar ideas, and they were two of the political agitators of the county."

Driven by anger, full of resentment, their minds shaped by vulgar Populist politics, Frank and Lou could have stepped out of the pages of any number of radical diatribes. Cather was not subtle about how unenlightened they were. Nor was she reticent about the power of Alexandra's enlightened, imaginative businesswoman's outlook. Cather's critics and scholars usually maintain that she had no interest in using her work to advance particular economic or social causes. "Economics and art are strangers," she once wrote and, while she lived in Greenwich Village for decades, she was never for a moment involved with its avant-garde culture or its socialist, Communist, and anarchist subcultures. But, as will become clearer in later chapters, the contrasts she presented in *O Pioneers!* were at the center of economic and social policy debates in 1913 America and, through Alexandra, she took a decidedly probusiness position which argued that successful immigrants, or at least successful immigrants in the country's heartland, were smart and forward-looking, not resentful dissidents who cast themselves as victims.

A Brief Note about Accomplished Women at the Turn of the Twentieth Century

In 1900, in its enumeration of the occupations of Americans, the US Census Bureau indicated that there were more than 300,000 women who were independent "farmers and planters." This was only a small percentage of the total 5.7 million people in the "farmer and planter" group. But it still indicates that, while rare, there were women who, like the fictional Alexandra, worked as full-fledged farmers.

Business-minded and entrepreneurial, practical, imaginative, an original thinker, the head of her family, single until she was almost 40, Cather's Alexandra Bergson was an example of what some commentators of the era called the "new woman." Arguably, other fictional characters also represent the general type: for example, Mary E. Wilkins Freeman's Louisa Ellis and Sarah Penn, Sarah Orne Jewett's Sylvia, Theodore Dreiser's Carrie Meeber, Kate Chopin's Agnes Pontellier, and a number of Edith Wharton's characters. In one way or another, all these characters refused the roles that had been prescribed for them, forged their own paths to freedom, and resisted efforts to rein them in. Alexandra Bergson was unique, however, because she did not rebel but was selected for her role by her father, because her values at least partially represented the values of the American business culture, and because her path, by design and in effect, was aimed at advancing the material well-being of her community, not just at securing her own freedom.

Many actual famous women of the era between the Civil War and World War I rebelled against conventional roles and, overcoming resistance, moved successfully into public life. I cannot do much more than name names here and suggest to my readers that they seek out details of their lives in such sources as the online database *American National Biography*.

In the Temperance movement, there was Frances Willard and Carry Nation. In the suffrage movement, the long effort to get the vote for women, there was Elizabeth Cady Stanton and Susan B. Anthony. Victoria Woodhull was the first female stockbroker on Wall Street, the first woman to run for President, and an important figure in the "free love" movement as well as other social reform movements. Ellen Richards, trained at MIT, led the domestic science and home economics movement. M. Carey Thomas, the long-time President of Bryn Mawr College, was an important innovator in higher education. "Mother" Mary Jones, Emma Goldman, and Elizabeth Gurley Flynn were among the most important and effective labor agitators and organizers. Margaret Anderson, Jane Heap, Harriet Munro, and Amy Lowell were key editors and leaders in the development of Modernist literature. Jane Addams was widely respected for her leadership of the "settlement house" movement, the suffrage movement, and her involvement in various reform efforts. She was probably the most widely known and respected of all these women.

Did these famous women have common characteristics? Yes. First, whether educated or not, they all developed expertise in their fields. Second, they all had highly developed writing and speaking skills. Third, they were charismatic. Fourth, they were not stopped by resistance from their families and communities. Fifth, they were typically not involved, at least during the major parts of their careers, in conventional relationships as spouses. Instead, many had other women as life partners, or spoke out forcefully for "free love," or believed in "serial monogamy," as Emma Goldman described it, or were not at all interested in the conventions of sex, marriage, and family.

4

Countrysides

The Context

Beginning shortly after the Civil War, American cities went through a long period of growth. Between 1870 and 1890, according to the US Census Bureau, New York City's population grew from 942,000 to more than 1.5 million, Chicago's grew from about 300,000 to one million, and Philadelphia's grew from 700,000 to one million. Smaller cities such as Baltimore, Boston, and Brooklyn (which was still separate from New York) at least doubled in size. In 1870, there were 14 cities with more than 100,000 residents; in 1890, there were 22. The growth of cities continued for several more decades.

Because of the availability of industrial jobs, many cities became primary immigrant destinations. In 1890, the total foreign-born population of the US was 9.3 million (that is, 14.8% of the total 62.6 population). About 40 percent of the 9.3 million foreign-born population lived in big cities. Major seaboard industrial centers, plus Chicago, were the most "foreign" of places: 42 percent of New Yorkers, 44 percent of Chicagoans, 35 percent of Bostonians, 33 percent of Brooklynites, and 26 percent of Philadelphians were born in other countries. The children of foreign-born parents – a substantial number, given the relatively high birthrates of first-generation immigrants – were not counted in these percentages. A common rule of thumb was that if there were three people on a city street, one would be a person born in another country, one would be the child of foreign parents, and one would be a "native" (that is, by the contemporary definition, a person whose family had been in the US for more than a generation).

The availability of industrial jobs might also have been expected to attract blacks to northern cities. In 1890, the total "Colored" population of the country – "Colored" referred mostly to African-Americans – was 7.5

million (that is, 12% of the population of 62.6 million). Of these, 90 percent lived in the old Confederate states. Only 1.7 percent of New Yorkers, 1.4 percent of Chicagoans, 3.8 percent of Philadelphians, 1.3 percent of Brooklynites, and 1.9 percent of Bostonians were "Colored." Other large industrial cities had even smaller "Colored" populations. For example, Milwaukee had 467 in its population of 204,000 and Buffalo had 1,100 in its population of 285,000. Southern cities had higher concentrations: in 1890, 26.4 percent of New Orleans' 242,000 residents, 27.8 percent of Louisville's 101,000 residents, and 32.5 percent of Washington's 230,000 residents were "Colored." The migration of southern blacks northward was a fairly slow process in general. By 1920, significant numbers of blacks had moved into northern cities, but even in 1940, more than 75 percent of blacks still lived in the South.

Some commentators of the era argued that the US was becoming an "urban" nation and that the countryside was being depopulated. To make this case, they cited Census statistics regarding the growth of the "urban" population from 25 percent in 1870, to 40 percent in 1900, to 57 percent in 1930. "Urbanization" was of course good news to many people because it was associated with progress, economic opportunity, and "modern" ways. In popular usage, "urban" meant "city."

By "urban," however, the Census Bureau did not mean "city." Rather, it defined "urban" as "cities and other incorporated places having 2,500 inhabitants or more." The Bureau's statistical threshold for declaring a place urban changed downward over time: in 1874, it had claimed that the threshold was 8,000 inhabitants, in 1880 it said the number was 4,000, then in 1890 and for many decades afterward, it used 2,500 as its threshold.

The basic point here is that when the Census Bureau said that 25 or 40 or 57 percent of Americans lived in "urban" places, it did not mean that they lived in cities. It meant only that that percentage lived in incorporated places, towns, villages, boroughs, and so forth which had at least 2,500 people. It did not mean that a person living, say, in a town of 3,000 in farmland Ohio or Mississippi was a "city" person, or that a person living on a farm within the boundaries of a Nebraska town of 2,600 was a "city" person. The distinction was lost on many commentators, then and now.

The Census Bureau provided decade-by-decade data regarding the "100 largest cities" which, when read carefully, corrected misunderstandings about "urbanization." Those data indicate that in 1870 about 18 percent of the American population lived in the 100 largest cities, that there was growth to 21 percent in 1890, to 23 percent in 1900, to 26 percent in 1910, and to almost 30 percent in 1940. The rate of city population growth significantly exceeded the rate of national population growth. The country's population doubled between 1870 and 1900, from 38.6 million to 76.2 million, while the populations of the 100 largest cities grew by more than 150 percent; the country's population grew by about 75 percent between 1900 and 1940, from 76.2 million to 132 million, while the populations of the 100 largest cities more than doubled.

Some of the 100 largest cities were, in fact, not so large: in 1870, for example, 60 had fewer than 40,000 inhabitants and 40 had fewer than 20,000, while in 1940, about half of the 100 largest had fewer than 150,000 inhabitants. Moreover, a "city" life could vary dramatically. People in 1900 or 1920 living in small cities like Chattanooga, Tennessee, or Tulsa, Oklahoma, or Utica, NY, each of which was among the 100 largest, probably had an entirely different life experience and lifestyle than people living in Chicago or Philadelphia or New York and may not have even acknowledged their "cityness." Someone living in a small manufacturing city with no downtown and no entertainment except saloons probably did not think of that place as a great city. Likewise, a 1900 resident of an immigrant ghetto in Manhattan or Philadelphia or Chicago, or a black person living in one of those cities in 1940, may never have even seen the man-made wonders that tourists wrote home about or have otherwise shared in the excitement of the new that was denoted by "city."

Trying to come to terms with city–country differences, the Census Bureau developed the concept of "metropolitan districts." In 1930, the Bureau stipulated that all communities that had a population density of more than 150 people per square mile, and that were adjacent and contiguous to cities of more than 50,000 people, were part of metropolitan areas. Even if people lived on farms or in small towns or in tiny villages on the city periphery, they were "metropolitans" by this definition. In 1930, 40 percent of Americans lived in metropolitan districts, according to the Bureau. Almost half of that 40 percent lived in the districts of Boston, New York/Northeastern New Jersey, Philadelphia, Chicago, and Los Angeles.

Some readers appreciate the explanatory power of numbers, while others can get lost in them. I will therefore summarize the three most important points that have been made so far:

1. The US population more than tripled from 38.6 million to 132 million between 1870 and 1940.

2. "Urban" and "city" are *not* synonyms, at least in Census Bureau usage, and "urbanization" statistics can mislead.
3. The population of the 100 largest American cities was 18 percent of the total population in 1870, 23 percent in 1900, 26 percent in 1910, and 30 percent in 1940.

Cities were not understood by some contemporaries simply as masses of people and jobs. They were understood as the central sites of the country's rapidly advancing commercial, technological, industrial, and financial power and as centers of artistic, intellectual, and lifestyle breakthroughs. They were metaphors for the modern and for American progress and power. In those respects, some cities became astonishing places. The first skyscraper was built in Chicago in 1885 and, over the next two generations, downtowns soared skyward. Beautiful downtown department stores served as palaces of merchandising and consumerism. Mansions and enormous, tasteful apartment buildings lined the major streets of some downtown areas. New transportation systems – first horse-pulled omnibuses, then street railways, then electric trolleys, and then giant subway and elevated rail systems in New York, Philadelphia, and Chicago – allowed the increasing populations to move out to new city neighborhoods, where they could take up residence in new housing units while continuing to work in other areas. Great new urban parks offered recreation amid delightful landscapes. Engineering triumphs like the Brooklyn Bridge became public symbols. City electrification changed the way many people, especially the young, thought of night and day.

The human possibilities of cities were also widely understood. One of the core life narratives of turn-of-the-twentieth-century Americans featured the person born and raised on a farm or in a small town who later migrated to some large city and became famous and perhaps rich. This narrative reflected the actual life experience of countless businesspeople, inventors, politicians, officials, scientists, artists, and writers. Big cities were their frontiers, full of like-minded people, useful social networks, excitement, and opportunity.

One of the less positive consequences of so much city development and expanding business opportunities was the steep increase in opportunities for politicians and their friends to get rich. Every major city of the era went through periods when newspapers reported on politicians dispensing patronage jobs to their contributors and other friends, taking kickbacks, taking bribes from businessmen for passing favorable ordinances, taking money to look the other way while prostitution and gambling thrived, selling the right to use city streets to trolley operators, selling the rights to provide gas and water to residents and businesses, and staying in their very profitable offices by fixing elections. Corrupt politicians existed at every level of government. Mark Twain's and Charles Dudley Warner's *The Gilded Age* (1873) was a satire that focused on corruption among US Congressmen. Walt Whitman remarked in *Democratic Vistas* (1872) that government at all levels, including the judiciary, was "saturated in corruption, bribery, falsehood, mal-administration." But it was city corruption that drew the most attention. There were constant newspaper reports, constant reform movements aimed at cleaning up corruption. The most famous piece of investigative journalism of the era was Lincoln Steffens's *The Shame of the Cities* (1904), which had chapters on St Louis, Minneapolis, Pittsburgh, Philadelphia, Chicago, and New York.

Compared to cities, rural America, except for mining and lumber boom-towns, was often said (mostly by city sophisticates) to be devoid of opportunity, isolated, and retrograde. Some city dwellers, not even attempting to disguise their contempt, spoke and wrote about the countryside as a sprawling wasteland full of coarse, ignorant hayseeds and other "hillbillies," while also claiming that small towns were populated entirely by unrelentingly dull, dumb, boring, narrow-minded, antimodern, and repressive people. Some of these beliefs were conveyed in the great number of jokes and smutty stories that circulated about rural folk, many featuring traveling salesmen and lonely farmers' wives, farmers consorting with farm animals, and country bumpkins getting hilariously bamboozled on trips into the city. There were serious commentaries, too. Frederick C. Howe, an important political reformer, summarized many of the conventional beliefs of city sophisticates in his autobiography, *The Confessions of a Reformer* (1925). Growing up in Meadville, Pennsylvania, Howe said, he and everyone else had been subjected to a "morality of duty, of careful respectability." He "had no rights as to my own life; danger lurked in doing what I wanted, even though what I wanted was innocent." The individual was taught what to think, how to behave, how to get on in the world by having associations with proper people and not "with men of questionable opinions." Howe did not explore, nor did writers of similar critiques, the ways in which the insularity and intolerance of small town people differed from the insularity and intolerance that could be found in any city neighborhood dominated by a particular ethnic or religious or socioeconomic group.

The great majority of later nineteenth- and earlier twentieth-century Americans continued to live on farms or in one of the country's tens of thousands of small towns, villages, hamlets, crossroads settlements, and nominal "cities" which did not make the Census Bureau's "100 largest" list. Here it should be recalled that only 18 percent of the total population in 1870, 23 percent in 1900, 26 percent in 1910, and 30 percent in 1940 lived in the country's "100 largest cities."

What did it mean to be a "rural" American? What was the "rural" experience? Those are complicated questions. They are complicated especially because the vast US subcontinent contains several distinct regions (the eastern seaboard, the South, the prairies, the western frontier, the Southwest, and so forth), a great number of subregions within each region, and many other forms of pronounced geographic and demographic variety. In sum, there were many rural Americas.

There were, for example, wide variations among communities in different regions of the US. There were deep differences among old eastern seaboard towns; Appalachian mountain towns; towns ancillary to the mining, forestry, and cattle industries; Great Plains communities built as service centers for settlers; southwestern and far western communities; and southern towns. The core enterprise of rural America, farming, also varied dramatically across regions and subregions. All farmers used land and required sun, water, and labor. That much – or that little – could be said. But there was little commonality between cotton, rice, and tobacco farming in the South, northeastern dairy farming, midwestern grain farming, western cattle ranching, and California truck farming.

Aside from regional economic differences, some of the variations among small towns, and in the buildings and layouts of the farmlands, were a consequence of the prevailing architectural fashions that existed when a particular place was built up. Other variations were a consequence of immigrant settlement patterns, with immigrant groups reproducing in whole or in part the familiar building forms of the old country. Still other variations resulted from the building materials available in particular places. Stone and brick buildings gave towns an air of solidity and permanence; wooden buildings could be worked by good carpenters into highly decorated forms, but wooden buildings could also be built cheaply, with the expectation that they were temporary houses for temporary residents.

The variable countryside was unstable in terms of its population. People migrated from region to region and within regions. Country people left for cities, city people went back home to the country, easterners moved westward, southern blacks moved north, and so forth. Signs of quick population shifts could be seen everywhere. Some New England places, for instance, grew rapidly, prospered, then were largely abandoned as their residents moved on to greener pastures. Boom towns in the West lasted just so long as the boom lasted, until, for example, all the gold and silver had been mined.

There were also, of course, stable places. Many towns housing local governments, for example, with significant numbers of local officials, judges, lawyers, businesspeople, and professionals, were showcases of the rural good life across generations. More of the good life was on display in suburban communities for the well-to-do, which began to develop on the edges of major cities in the last years of the nineteenth century. Reflecting the interest in high English culture among their residents, many of these small, exclusive new suburbs were built as English-style villages surrounded by country estates, with easy access to country clubs, yacht clubs, and golf clubs.

The Literature

Many writers understood that local environments shaped character, established outlooks, and defined individual possibilities. Examining local environments, then, could be a means by which to explore the quality of American life, and telling the story of a character in a "typical" American environment could be a focused way of testing the truth of perennial pronouncements about the country's progress, decency, and wholesomeness. Telling such stories could also be a means by which to explore what virtually everyone of the period seemed to agree about, that the US was unified in a number of ways but that people continued to live within and to be shaped by local cultures, that they had little contact with ideas or people that were not local. Given the tremendous geographical and cultural differences in the country, defining what was "typical" or "representative," extrapolating truths about the country as a whole from stories, was at least problematic and maybe impossible.

Locally focused countryside writing of the years from 1865 to 1929 that is still widely read includes the New England work of Sarah Orne Jewett, Mary E. Wilkins Freeman, Robert Frost, and Edith Wharton and the upper Midwest work of Hamlin Garland, Willa Cather, and Sherwood Anderson. Much of this work was set in farmlands that were notoriously difficult to cultivate and in the towns and villages that served those farmlands. For example, the actual New England farmlands that writers like Freeman and Frost knew had short growing seasons, too many rocks, too little topsoil, and too many hills and mountains; farm abandonment and migration out of those areas to other regions of the country began early in their history and continued into the twentieth century. The actual western Wisconsin farmlands that Garland knew had similar problems, and Cather's Nebraska farmlands posed different but parallel difficulties to all farmers except the most innovative, as *O, Pioneers!* suggested. In all these places, of course, the destinies of towns and villages were tied to their surrounding farmlands. If the farms prospered, so did the towns; when the farms failed, the towns failed.

City literature was just as locally focused as the literature of the countryside. That is, this literature represented life not in large diverse places but in small, insular neighborhoods or blocks within neighborhoods. Lower Manhattan, the few densely populated square miles bordered on the north by Fourteenth Street and including Little Italy, Chinatown, and the Lower East Side, was the setting of much of the literature by and about immigrants and lower-working-class people. Stephen Crane's *Maggie: A Girl of the Streets*, which includes scenes in a tenement, in a few saloons and clubs, and on a few lower Manhattan streets, is typical of such writing. Greenwich Village, the area between Fourteenth Street and the immigrant neighborhoods, was a center for art, writing, and dissident politics through much of the early twentieth century, but the city writing of Villagers was almost uniformly about life among Village artists and would-be artists who rarely traveled beyond their neighborhoods. The same local focus can be found in city literature representing life in the upper classes. In Edith Wharton's Manhattan fictions, for instance, there was almost nothing that suggested that there was life beyond the uptown drawing rooms and opera houses populated by the wealthy. Theodore Dreiser's *Sister Carrie* (1900) was perhaps the most comprehensive of city novels. But even that great book only includes scenes in a few Chicago neighborhoods, a few Manhattan residential neighborhoods, in the Broadway theatre district, and in a small section of Brooklyn.

I have discussed and will discuss city-focused literature in other chapters. Here, I want to briefly comment on some of the classic countryside literature of the era. Because the locale of so much twentieth-century American literature continued to be the countryside, these comments should be understood not as "covering" the subject but as introducing it.

Picture-perfect farmhouses surrounded by beautiful, carefully tended fields and highlighted by well-placed landscaping existed in many farming communities blessed with good soil, decent weather, and access to markets. The sort of farm that Alexandra in *O, Pioneers!* created out of nothing was a representation of one of those, as was, presumably, the house and vineyards that the narrator of "The Goophered Grapevine" brought back from ruin. Likewise, the flawless houses surrounded by lovely gardens that existed in many small towns were represented in novels such as Cather's *My Antonia* and in some New England fiction such as Sarah Orne Jewett's "Martha's Lady," an 1897 story set in a "the best house in a quiet New England village" with its "large sunshiny garden" full of red and white peonies, golden lilies, and blue larkspurs. The promise of settled, decent, wholesome, good living was conveyed in such images, and in the minds of contemporary readers those images must have taken on very large meanings about human possibility and the graciousness of the good life.

But the houses and landscapes usually pictured in the classic American literature of the countryside were ugly and flimsy testimonies to hardship and human limitations. New human settlements on the prairies, such as appeared in Hamlin Garland's fiction and memoirs, often seemed to be very temporary and insubstantial. In Garland's first collection of stories, *Main-Travelled Roads* (1891), farms were described as slovenly, as if the owners had been overcome by the sheer toil of maintaining them. The house of the farm family in "Up the Coulé," for example, was described as:

> a small white house, story-and-a-half structure, with a wing, set in the middle of a few locust trees; a small drab-colored barn, with a sagging ridge-pole; a barnyard full of mud, in which a few cows were standing, fighting the flies and waiting to be milked. An old man was pumping water at the well; the pigs were squealing from a pen nearby; a child was crying.

Similar houses appear constantly in New England fiction. In the 1891 "The Revolt of 'Mother,'" Mary E. Wilkins Freeman's brilliant story, a wife has suffered for 40 years raising a family and doing her chores in a tiny house in which the best room is described as having no carpet and dirty wallpaper, even though her husband, who has done well at farming, is building a great barn for his livestock. In Sarah Orne Jewett's "A White Heron," the house in which the girl Sylvie and her grandmother live is described, from the point of view of the intruding bird collector, as a tiny, clean "hermitage," which is a welcome surprise to him because in his travels in the New England "wilderness" he has known "the horrors of its most primitive housekeeping, and the dreary squalor of that level of society which does not rebel at the companionship of hens." The sort of squalor – rural New England slums, more or less – alluded to in Jewett's story was pictured in Edith Wharton's novel *Summer* (1917). That novel, like Wharton's earlier novella *Ethan Frome* (1911), contains penetrating descriptions of town and country life and landscapes. Wharton was acutely aware of variations within the New England landscape, and *Summer* includes descriptions of Greek Revival houses that have become decrepit, sleepy villages and bleak hamlets, a lively small town, and a community of mountain farmers who live in "savage misery" in houses that "were hardly more than sheds, built of logs and rough boards, with tin stove-pipes sticking out of their roofs."

Grim landscapes sometimes produce dazed, debauched people. In *Summer*, the mountain farmers are filthy, "drink-dazed" folk who seem to have been "herded together in a sort of passive promiscuity in which their common misery was the strongest link." Sometimes the landscape forces a character into a recognition of actuality, as when, near the end of Garland's "Up the Coulé," the sister-in-law of the main character speaks of the narrowness of farm life, saying "It's nothing but fret, fret and work the whole time, never going any place, never seeing anybody but a lot of neighbors just as big fools as you are. I spend my time fighting flies and washing dishes and churning [butter]. I'm sick of it all." She would leave for a city if she were a man, she says. But the narrator of the story undercuts that dream a few paragraphs later, when he says that "She didn't know that the struggle for a place to stand on this planet was eating the heart and soul out of men and women in the city, just as in the country." Sometimes, though, characters reach out for justice and dignity, as when Jewett's Sylvie resists the temptations of the intruder and protects the white heron, or when Freeman's "Mother" finally rebels and gains a victory over her husband (to whom she remains dutiful, however), and as when some of Garland's characters talk seriously about trying to bring about political changes that will relieve some of their burdens.

The lives of ordinary New England and midwestern country people represented in the classic literature were often as dreary and empty as the landscapes. Work, family, community life, and modes of expression – the basic elements and building blocks of lives – are usually described as deficient or nonexistent. At best in this fiction, work is overwhelmingly monotonous and difficult, but in many stories real work simply does not exist, leading readers to wonder what many of these characters actually do with themselves. The lack of work or the sheer drudgery of the work drives many to leave the countryside for greener pastures, and families are often depicted as broken or dysfunctional. In many stories, children die early or leave for other parts of the country, never or rarely to return. Family relationships in Freeman's "Mother" are painful. Jewett's Sylvie in "A White Heron" left her siblings behind when she was rescued by her grandmother from life in a manufacturing town; the grandmother "had buried four children, so Sylvia's mother, and a son (who might be dead in California) were all the children she had left." Similar painful, broken family situations exist in Wharton's *Summer* and throughout Garland's Midwest fictions. Moreover, communities of people connected by similar interests, kinship, social goals, and so forth, are rarely seen in this fiction, except in cases when a group of people come together to express their distaste at the unusual behavior of individuals and thereby assert community standards.

Not surprisingly, writers often represent and assess their characters by how articulate they are, how they can connect with others through language, how they can translate or express their inner desires in words, and so forth. In the literature of the countryside, there is mostly silence. In *Ethan Frome* and *Summer* there are long silences broken by a few words here and there; in "The Revolt of 'Mother,'" the husband's speech was "almost as inarticulate as a growl," the son is learning his language from the father, and Mother hears it as "her most native tongue." In another great story by Freeman, "A New England Nun," a long relationship ends "tenderly" but with very few words as the woman returns "like a queen" to her happy life of well-ordered solitude and silence.

A sense of solitude, if not aloneness, and of vast silences or minimal articulation is characteristic of a great deal of Robert Frost's poetry. Contemplative poems such as "Mowing," "The Road Not Taken," "An Old Man's Winter Night," "Stopping by Woods on a Snowy Evening," "Design," and "Directive" are brief utterances made by solitary people who inhabit silent landscapes. "Directive," full of details found in the rubble and cellar holes of its abandoned towns, includes some imagined interaction with long-gone people. Many of Frost's other contemplative poems indicate no human interaction at all, while his narrative poems involve terse exchanges, repetitions of the same words, inarticulateness, and only occasionally, as in "The Death of the Hired Man" and "Home Burial," extended exchanges of ideas and perceptions.

Silence can mean many things. It can mean depression and disengagement from surroundings, it can indicate that a character living a routinized life simply has nothing to say, it can signal anger. In Frost, though, silence or terseness often suggests careful consideration, a healthy distrust of slippery words, and, most of all, self-containment. That self-containment is one of two sources of the dignity of his countryside people. The other is the fact that they do work that matters to them, that is sometimes beautiful, and that others understand and respect. That kind of work exists in some of the most anthologized of Frost poems: it can be found in the whispering scythe of "Mowing," in the brotherly labor of "The Tuft of Flowers," in the insights derived from fixing a stone fence in "Mending Wall," in the pride Silas takes in his labor in "The Death of a Hired Man," in the cherishing of product and the deep effect of work processes on the speaker in "After Apple-Picking," in the soulful wood-splitting and uniting of vocation and avocation in "Two Tramps in Mud-Time," in the vitality of workers in "The Line-Gang," in the love of craft and well-wrought tools in "The Ax-Helve." As we shall see in the next chapters, running through the history of the 1865–1929 period were profound and disturbing disputes about soulless work, work that was only done for pay, and the exploitation of the working classes. I can think of no writer of the time other than Frost who wrote about physical work enthusiastically done by workers. The significance of this may not be clear to readers at this point, but it will be later.

The most singular, most famous early twentieth-century fiction focused on the countryside was Sherwood Anderson's collection of linked stories, *Winesburg, Ohio* (1919). Most of *Winesburg*'s characters work very little; of those that do work, only one, the insane patriarch Jesse Bentley of "Godliness," seems to care about it. This disengagement with work, or nonengagement, however, is only a small part of what makes up the sad, isolated, hopeless, sexually repressed, compulsion-driven or fear-driven or terror-stricken lives of Anderson's characters. In a few instances in *Winesburg* there is some sunshine that penetrates the dark lives, some temporary relief, a connection between people, a sexual encounter (almost always remembered with guilt). But most of its brilliantly executed stories read like case studies of psychological disorders, which Anderson may, in part, have intended them to be. Like a number of other writers of the time, he was influenced by his understanding of how the new psychological theories of Sigmund Freud explained human character and behavior patterns and sometimes understood his own creations in Freudian terms.

The kind of negative silence that is present in the work of Freeman and Jewett, Garland and Wharton pervades *Winesburg*. Along with quiet murmurs, it can be heard in the four most widely read stories, "Hands," "Mother," "Adventure," and "Queer." In "Hands," Wing Biddlebaum, called "Biddlebaum the silent," is said to have lived "long years of silence" punctuated by occasional manic outbursts of talk to the one person with whom he has contact, George Willard, and by memories of the screams and roars of the homophobic people who drove him into his isolation. In "Mother," Elizabeth Willard does a lot of murmuring and whispering to herself, spends many of her long days "staring out over the tin roofs into the main street of Winesburg," and is sometimes joined in that activity by her son, George (who often talks aloud to himself), with whom she mostly sits in silence; all of her passive behavior camouflages her fury and her sometimes murderous feelings. In "Adventure," Alice Hindman has been waiting in utter loneliness for several years for her lover who left for Cleveland. "She was very quiet," the narrator says, "but beneath a placid exterior a continual ferment went on." Like Elizabeth Willard, Alice whispers and mutters to herself. "Adventure" ends when she runs naked into the dark night; she is apparently in search of a man but finds only an old man who was "somewhat deaf." In "Queer," Elmer Cowley is a new resident of the town. No one in the town talks to him, he lashes out constantly and furiously and seems to relate only to Mook, a "half wit" farm laborer who is most articulate when talking to farm animals (there are several other "half-wits" in *Winesburg*). Elmer's story ends with his enraged assault on George Willard, who has done nothing to him, and his statement that "I guess I showed him. I ain't no queer. I guess I showed him I ain't no queer." ("Queer," incidentally, sometimes referred to homosexuality in the early twentieth century but more often meant odd or peculiar.)

Most of Winesburg's characters suffer from some kind of phobia, sexual repression, fixation, guilt, religious fantasy, and so forth. Virtually none of them have any dignity. Some, like Alice, Elizabeth, and Wing end up, literally, on their knees at key moments. Elmer Cowley's father, Dr Reefy of "Paper Pills," Dr Parcival of "The Philosopher," and Wash Williams of "Respectability" live in filthy rooms or wear the same filthy clothes for years on end. A few spend much of their time morosely sitting in front of their windows staring into the empty streets. Some, including Elizabeth and Wing, age prematurely.

Some of Anderson's characters were born in Winesburg, others had migrated to it from other towns and cities, and some were preparing to leave. Their different origins and destinations were perhaps Anderson's way of suggesting that psychologically troubled people existed everywhere in the US or, more generally, that "modern" people were inevitably unbalanced. But, whatever the case, *Winesburg* is a book that depicts an American small town – or *the* small town, enthusiastic readers have always said – as a disturbed, soulless, deadly, silent asylum for misfits.

The most encyclopedic and sociologically accurate of all the literature concerning the early twentieth-century small town was Sinclair Lewis's novel *Main Street* (1920). Lewis's protagonist, Carol Kennicott, a recent graduate of a St. Paul, Minnesota college who works as a librarian in that city, marries a medical doctor who resides in the 3,000-person community of Gopher Prairie. Carol arrives in the town with ideas, learned at college and in books, about what a small town should look like and what values its residents should endorse. Finding a typical undistinguished, provincial town full of conformist people, Carol sets out to reform it. Over several years, she fails in every one of her efforts to get the local leading citizens to beautify the town, to change their manners, to improve their reading and entertainment habits, to see the wisdom of her broad-minded thinking about labor and social change, and so forth. Lewis, a great satirist, is nearly as skeptical of Carol's high-minded, fashionable projects as he is of the low-minded, hypocritical, incurious local folk. But Carol has nothing of the meanness of the local culture which, as in Anderson and others, is shown to have deep hostilities to outsiders and terrifying propensities to brutally hammer down, as an old Japanese saying goes, any nail that sticks out.

5

The Poor and the Wealthy

The Context

At the beginning of his *Progress and Poverty* (1879), the political economist Henry George remarked on the central "paradox" of the nineteenth century. On the one hand, George wrote, "The march of invention has clothed mankind with powers of which a century ago the boldest imagination could not have dreamed." On the other hand, he said:

> in factories where laborsaving machinery has reached its most wonderful development, little children are at work; wherever the new forces are anything like fully utilized, large classes are maintained by charity or live on the verge of recourse to it; amid the greatest accumulations of wealth, men die of starvation, and puny infants suckle dry breasts; while everywhere the greed of gain, the worship of wealth, shows the force of the fear of want.

For George, who drew a good deal of his evidence from the American situation and especially from the state of affairs in New York City and in his native San Francisco, widespread poverty in the midst of progress was "the central fact from which spring industrial, social, and political difficulties that perplex the world, and with which statesmanship and philanthropy and education grapple in vain."

Henry George was a reform-minded economist and might therefore have been expected to emphasize what he called the "misery and wretchedness" of the masses. But his understanding was widely shared. Andrew Carnegie, who had begun as a poor immigrant boy from Scotland and who rose to become the titan of the American steel industry and one of the richest men of his time, acknowledged the existence of a pervasive "caste" system in his 1889 essay, "Wealth," though, unlike others, he "welcomed" inequality as "essential for the progress of the [human] race." Jacob Riis's *How the Other Half Lives* (1890) presented prose and photographic evidence of immigrant poverty in downtown Manhattan; Riis was also a popular speaker on the subject. Perhaps the most widely read general description of inequality was in the first chapter of Edward Bellamy's *Looking Backward* (1887), which described a society in which hordes of toilers, suffering the "pitiless lashing of hunger," struggled to pull a carriage on which sat a very few comfortable people who constantly feared that they might lose their seats and who suffered from a "singular hallucination … that they were not exactly like their brothers and sisters who pulled at the rope, but of finer clay." Bellamy's novel influenced the thinking of two generations of reformers. To a somewhat lesser but still significant extent, so did Edward Markham's "The Man with the Hoe." Markham's poem first appeared in the San Francisco *Examiner* in January, 1899 and was then reprinted in several hundred US and Canadian newspapers. It described a worker who, carrying the burdens of the world on his shoulders, had been reduced to something "stolid and stunned, a brother to the ox" and whose "dread shape" represented "humanity betrayed / Plundered, profaned, and disinherited."

Inequality existed everywhere, of course, not only in the United States. This fact was recognized in the 1891 encyclical written by Pope Leo XIII. In *De Rerum Novarum* ("Of New Things"), subtitled "Rights and Duties of Capital and Labor," Pope Leo remarked on the tremendous recent growth of industry and the changed relations of "masters and workmen," the "enormous fortunes of some few individuals, and the utter poverty of the working classes." The result of this situation, he said, was overwhelming danger to human harmony brought on by conflicts between labor and capital, danger to the "natural rights" of private property holders from angry revolutionary socialists, danger to public order, and danger to moral order. Throughout the lengthy encyclical, which became the foundation document of Roman Catholic teaching on modern social justice, there was a sharp recognition of the need for a remedy "for the misery and wretchedness pressing so unjustly on the majority of the working class" who had been "surrendered, isolated and helpless, to the hardheartedness of employers and the greed of unchecked competition."

Economic inequality in the US, as elsewhere, persisted across decades. National attention to economic inequality as a fundamental American reality and as the immediate cause of other problems ebbed and flowed.

The late nineteenth century was a flow time of national attention. The years between 1910 and 1919 were a period of *torrential* flow. Measured by what was euphemistically called "industrial unrest," that is, high numbers of strikes, lockouts, riots, and outbreaks of violence, many of which resulted in martial law declarations, those years were in fact, arguably, the most threatening to national order of any since the Civil War. In 1912, President Woodrow Wilson and Congress responded to the "unrest" by establishing the United States Congressional Commission on Industrial Relations to study its causes. The Commission spent three years gathering social and economic data, analyzing those data, and holding hearings. Its large staff of experts produced graphs, tables, summaries of testimony, analyses of particular data, and more general reports. In 1916, the Commission issued its findings and its recommendations in 11 thick volumes.

In its summary of its findings, the Commissioners argued that "industrial unrest" was essentially the result of high unemployment, a court system that was deeply prejudiced against working people, the fact that workers were prevented from forming unions that could negotiate fair wages and working conditions with employers, and, most importantly and fundamentally, the inequitable distribution of wealth and income. Shocking its readers, the Commission reported that, based on the work of a statistician of "conservative views," the richest 2 percent of the US population owned 60 percent of the nation's wealth, the 33 percent of the population that was middle class owned 35 percent of the wealth, and the 65 percent of the population that was poor owned 5 percent of the wealth. This breakdown, it should be noted, reflected the nation's situation from 1912 to 1915, years which, while marked by "unrest," were relatively robust in terms of most economic measures.

Significant numbers of Americans believed, and would continue to believe, that poverty was self-created, that the poor were lazy, immoral, unfit, alcohol-dependent, and resistant to work. That is, according to this way of thinking, the poor were to blame for their poverty; they were victims of their own bad behavior. However, using empirical data, the Industrial Relations Commission reported that in reality the poor were people who worked long hours under sometimes brutal conditions but were not paid enough to make ends meet. Who, then, were the poor? They were, largely, the "working poor" and their families.

The 1916 Commission report contained a great number of descriptions and analyses of social conditions in the United States. Among its most important and widely discussed findings were the following:

- Industrial relations, the relationship of employees and employers, shaped what a man and his family "shall eat, what they shall wear, how many hours of his life he shall labor and in what surroundings." As a rule, industrial relations in the US were imbalanced: employers controlled everything and employees were powerless. "Industrial feudalism" prevailed in many sectors of American manufacturing, mining, and agriculture.

- There had been a 188 percent increase in national wealth over the past 25 years, largely because of the labor of working people. But working people had "emphatically" not received a "fair share" of that increased wealth.

- At least one-third and possibly one-half of the families of workers employed in manufacturing and mining earned less than "enough to support them in anything like a comfortable and decent condition." Only one-quarter of working-class fathers earned enough to support their families; mothers and children were therefore forced to work, typically for wages significantly less than were paid to men.

- Thirty percent of worker families "kept boarders and lodgers, a condition repugnant to every ideal of family life, especially in the crowded tenements and tiny cottages in which the wage earners of America characteristically live. Furthermore, in 77 per cent of the families two or more persons occupied each sleeping room, in 37 per cent three or more persons, and in 15 per cent four or more persons." These statistics demonstrated that the nuclear family, the foundation of society, was under assault.

- Workers in the basic industries of the country were typically unemployed "for at least one-fifth of the year."

- Hazardous working conditions existed in many industries. On average, there had been 35,000 on-the-job deaths each year over the prior several decades. Deaths by work-related, degenerative disease (asbestosis, black lung disease, white lung disease, etc.) were not included in this average.

- For many workers, there was no dignity even in death. Many families could not afford proper burial. In New York City, "one out of twelve corpses is buried at the expense of the city or turned over to physicians for dissection."

- Infant mortality among the poor was high. For example, in the manufacturing city of Johnstown, Pennsylvania, infant mortality rates ranged up to 256 per 1,000 births in the families of poor workers, which was three times the rate experienced by children born into the families of well-paid workers.

- In six of the largest cities, "12 to 20 per cent of the children were noticeably underfed and ill-nourished."

- Only one-third of children completed elementary school. Less than 10 per cent finished high school. The dropouts "are almost entirely the children of the workers, who, as soon as they reach working age, are thrown, immature, ill-trained, and with no practical knowledge, into the complexities of industrial life."

- While no exact national figures were available regarding the conditions of agricultural laborers, "speaking generally, the available evidence indicates clearly that while in some sections agricultural laborers are well paid and fairly treated, the condition of the mass is very much like that of the industrial workers."

- Family farm ownership had been intimately associated with American well-being and opportunity, but "The most alarming fact in American agriculture was the rapid growth of tenancy." In 1910, 37 percent of farms were tenant-operated, as compared to 28 percent in 1890. There had been no national study of tenant farmer conditions, but a Texas study was cited: "Badly housed, ill-nourished, uneducated and hopeless, these tenants continue year after year to eke out a bare living, moving frequently from one farm to another in the hope that something will turn up."

A great deal of the energy of the Commission on Industrial Relations was devoted to the "working poor" because, angry and sometimes rebellious, they were the source of much of the era's "unrest." The least amount of the Commission's attention was paid to the middle class, though it was fairly clear that many of the reforms that the Commissioners suggested were aimed at moving underpaid workers up into respectable middle-class situations. The Commission's discussion of the rich was also brief but it was full of barely concealed outrage. Its most fundamental point was that, in contrast to the masses of poor people, there were 1,598 American "fortunes yielding an income of $100,000 or more per year" (that is, from investments) and there were 44 families with incomes of $1,000,000 or more per year. The largest fortune in the country, estimated at one billion dollars, equaled the aggregate wealth of 2.5 million of the people the Commission classified as poor. Carl Sandburg, who at the time was making his living as a Chicago reporter, wrote about the Commission's findings and, faced with the bureaucratic, statistical prose in which it was presented, "translated" it for his readers: "44 families pull down $1,000,000 or more. Most of these people don't work. They don't have to. The working class brings them everything they want and more than they can use."[1]

National attention to issues of inequality, as I indicated earlier, ebbed and flowed across time. The second decade of the twentieth century was a period of torrential flow, and the findings of the Industrial Relations Commission represented a particularly high point. It did not last long. After the US entered World War I in early 1917, attention to inequality ebbed. Moreover, for a number of reasons that will be discussed later, from World War I through the 1920s any expression of concern about inequality was alleged by defenders of the American way of life to be "foreign" and subversive.

There had always been deep hostility to the rich in the country. Dissident political parties were not reluctant to place the blame for inequality, and everything that inequality produced, on the rich. There were constant reports about how the financial and manufacturing titans paid big money to office-holders for favors (though it was usually the case that the office-holders insisted on being paid). Cresting around 1900, there was considerable public discussion about how the titans' cutthroat business practices drove out all competition in the course of creating monopolies that controlled many of the nation's basic goods and services. There were lots of cartoons of fat rich men clutching giant cigars while, for example, stepping on the throats of thin, bedraggled workers and children, The weird or miserly behavior of some rich people was gleefully reported. John D. Rockefeller's tough business and antilabor practices were legendary. After the 1890s, in what seems to have been an effort to express an opinion about Rockefeller's life-draining character, it was often alleged that, in an effort to keep up his strength, he drank mother's milk provided by lactating women he hired. There were accounts of the bizarre "conspicuous consumption" of rich people (the ironic phrase was economist Thorstein Veblen's in his 1899 *The Theory of the Leisure Class*), a form of consumption meant to put on public display the ownership of nonessential goods in order to demonstrate respectability and power. There were accounts of the profligate behavior of the children of the rich. The possibilities for excoriating the rich were virtually endless, and they were taken up.

---

[1] Carl Sandburg, "That Walsh Report," *International Socialist Review*, 11 (October 1915), p. 198.

But all that negative commentary was more than counterbalanced in popular culture, the publishing outlets of which were owned by the rich, by considerable respect or even adoration for the wealthy, attempts to imitate their behavior and tastes, and, most of all, by the efforts of countless individuals to somehow join the ranks of the wealthy. Year after year, there were great numbers of press reports on their behavior. Constant attention was paid to their travel plans, who was seen with whom, who was wearing what, whose party was astoundingly lavish, which clubs were meeting when, who was summering in what part of the country, whose child was making her formal debut, whose child was off to what fine college, who had died and how that person's final resting place was such a gorgeous part of the landscape. The food intake of big eaters like "Diamond" Jim Brady of New York was reported in newspapers. A constant subject was how this or that famous woman's hair was layered, curled, and swirled upward (or downward), how the treatment set off her fine features and lovely round arms (round arms, and sumptuous bodies generally, were "in" for many years). The phrases "diamonds are forever" and "diamonds are a girl's best friend" had not yet been coined, but reports of what diamonds a woman owned sometimes appeared, as in November 1885, when the *New York Times* published an article on how Senator Stanford of California (who was also the founder of Stanford University) had recently bought his wife four diamond necklaces that had been previously owned by Queen Isabella of Spain, paying more than $600,000 for them.[2] The Stanfords were not heard to protest such reportage as an invasion of privacy.

In their time, with few exceptions, the chief American industrialists pictured in news reports and "society" columns were idealized as people who began life in the lower classes and advanced through hard work. Their heroic stories were stated and restated. Men of tremendous power, they were sometimes given full biographical treatment. But brief sketches such as the following were recited in countless newspaper articles and speeches:

- Cornelius Vanderbilt was the son of a poor farmer. He hated schools and books and quit his formal education when he was 11, worked hard and rose up in the world, succeeded as a steamship and railroad scion, built a mansion a full block long on New York's Fifth Avenue, and developed one of the world's great private art collections. His son,

[2] "Mrs. Stanford's Diamonds; Over a Million in Brilliants," *New York Times*, November 22, 1885, p. 6.

William, who became a popular legend because of his railroad enterprises, doubled the $90 million he had been left by his father. His grandson, Cornelius, was also a great railroad magnate but was more widely known for his philanthropy, for his service as Chair of the Executive Committee of the Metropolitan Museum of Art and as a director of the American Museum of Natural History, and for his building of "The Breakers," the 70-room mansion decorated by a group of great artists and artisans on his summer estate in Newport, Rhode Island.

- Meyer Guggenheim began as an immigrant Jew from Switzerland, peddled small items and stove polish door to door in Philadelphia and other parts of Pennsylvania, was personable and understood business, began to produce the stove polish on his own after stealing the formula from the manufacturer, sold lots of it, invested in the lace business, bought and sold railroad stocks, saw great opportunities in Colorado mining towns, and, with his four smart sons as his partners, went into mine investment, then into ore smelting. The Guggenheims ultimately controlled all of the key US smelters, then began a series of mining and smelting investments in Mexico, in other parts of the Americas, and in other parts of the world.
- Andrew Carnegie began as a poor immigrant Scottish boy, worked his way up in the iron industry of western Pennsylvania, got capital, invested well, went into steel manufacturing, became one of the richest men in the world as the US became the world's greatest steel producer, and gave much of it back to the community through philanthropy.
- Henry Clay Frick, a partner of Carnegie, grew up as the son of a poor farmer, dropped out of a small college, saw that Pennsylvania coal, which could be turned into coke for the creation of steel, was the future, became the "coke king" of his time, seemed to his friends to be narrow and only interested in coke and steel, moved in 1906 to a mansion he built on Fifth Avenue, developed one of the world's great collections of European art, and when he died in 1919, left an estate of $142 million, $117 million of which went to philanthropies, and his art collection, valued at $50 million, which was given to New York City.

In a number of ways, such stories – and there were many others of local rich men which appeared in local newspapers – perfectly mirrored the values and character traits that many claimed were the popular American beliefs about human possibility. They showed that immigrants could be successful, that hard work and innovation paid off, that formal education was unnecessary, that a successful person could and should constantly take on new challenges, that successful men were benefactors of the community, and that many were sensitive to the finer things in life. Most of all, needless to say, they demonstrated that a person could move upward in society, that being born poor was no excuse for not moving up.

Written and spoken narratives about human possibility in the US had a large, appreciative audience. Visually, the presence and worth and power of the rich was also demonstrated. Social stratification in the US, as elsewhere, involves geographical determinism, the idea that people *are*, so to speak, where they reside and where they bring their families to reside. The multimillionaire class lived this principle. They built homes that were manifestations of their success.

City mansions that could be seen by passersby were said to help build "civic pride," in the standard newspaper phrase of the day. Because cities like New York, Chicago, and Philadelphia grew at such rapid rates, and residential districts occupied by the rich were periodically overtaken by commercial development (zoning as a planning tool was not yet in use), mansions and "millionaire rows" tended to be impermanent. For example, after Central Park in Manhattan was completed in the early 1870s, Fifth Avenue on the east side, facing the Park, was lined with the mansions of the superrich, each taking up a block or so of very expensive land (Henry Clay Frick paid $2,500,000 for his lot at Fifth Avenue and 70th Street in 1906). A generation later, by the early 1920s, many of the rich had moved out of the city into country estates, and many of their mansions had been demolished and replaced by high-end apartment buildings. But the impermanence of some city mansions mostly suggested that the superrich were on the move, a healthy thing, while the erection of large apartment buildings filled with lots of moderately rich people suggested that the ranks of the upper classes were expanding.

There were few places like Manhattan. In most large and small cities, small towns, county seats, and even in some rural farming and mining areas, "millionaire rows" were permanent installations. Mansions were usually designed by architects, built by highly skilled artisans, decorated by professionals, and landscaped by landscape architects. They were enormous in size with many specialized spaces such as libraries, billiard rooms, and attached greenhouses. They were obviously good, showy ways of spending money, good investments in social capital, and good ways of bringing fine artistic taste into ugly landscapes peopled by so many who did not have enough money for adequate food or clothing and who lived, in so many instances, in ugly or plain houses. Finally, they were demonstrations that there was a lot more to America than inequality and the resulting social ills.

Before I move on to comment on some of the literature focused on wealthy people, I should say something about the absence in the preceding account of two descriptive phrases long used by literary historians and others. One is the description of the titans of American industry as "robber barons." The phrase was first popularized by Matthew Josephson in his 1934 book *The Robber Barons: The Great American Capitalists, 1861–1901*, though the *OED* reports that it appeared earlier but not in regard to the titans. I have not used the phrase because I believe it leads away from an understanding of how widely honored the titans were in their own time and also because it is misleading to read back into history a later understanding of people and events. Of course, the titans were not universally honored. They were called lots of nasty things in their own time by dissidents, as we shall see in later chapters, but not "robber barons."

The second phrase that is absent from the preceding account is "Social Darwinism," the theory that only the "fit" survive, or *should* survive, in human society. While used before 1900 by Herbert Spencer and others, and later used in some arguments about white racial superiority, this phase was not often used in discussions of inequality or in regard to the titans, as evidenced by newspaper and magazine archives and the *OED*. For reasons similar to my nonuse of "robber barons," I have not used "Social Darwinism."

The Literature

Much American literature was focused on poor people, ordinary folk, common men and women. Representations of those sorts of people have been my subjects in my earlier discussions and they will be in later discussions. Here, I will concentrate on the representation of wealthy people.

They were not viewed sympathetically in most American literary classics. The dominant business culture was viewed as boring, inane, hurtful to the interests of ordinary people, obsessed with material comforts, and thoroughly unspiritual; businessmen were typically seen as narrow, materialistic, dumb, and heartless. Claims that there was substantial social mobility in the United States, and therefore great freedom, were viewed with considerable skepticism. Moreover, the logic of publicly displayed wealth – a logic stressing the idea that an individual is what he or she owns and must show it off – struck many writers as the most shallow and empty of philosophies.

Only one major writer, Theodore Dreiser, produced an even partially sympathetic portrait of a business titan. Dreiser's novels *The Financier* (1912) and *The Titan* (1914) were based on the life and business ventures of Charles Tyson Yerkes, Jr., who was known in his time as the king of streetcars, that is, trolley systems in various cities. Calling his character Frank Cowperwood, Dreiser included in his novels extremely detailed accounts of business practices, the relations between businessmen and politicians, the workings of markets, and maneuvers within the nation's financial systems. In addition, Dreiser focused on the passionate desires of the brilliant, amoral, tough-minded Cowperwood: his passion for women, his quest for acceptance in high society, his business triumphs, his assembling of his art collection, and his building of a great mansion as a "monument to his memory" and as a museum for his art acquisitions. Dreiser's detailed description in *The Titan* of Cowperwood's plan for the mansion/ museum begins: "The whole structure was to be of a rich brownstone, heavily carved. For its interior decoration the richest woods, silks, tapestries, glass, and marbles were canvassed. The main rooms were to surround a great central court with a colonnade of pink-veined alabaster, and in the center there would be an electrically lighted fountain of alabaster and silver." Behind his art collections and his grand architectural plans lay, according to Dreiser, not simple, vulgar conspicuous consumption but Cowperwood's love of art: "Of all individuals, he respected, indeed revered, the sincere artist. Existence was a mystery, but these souls who set themselves to quiet tasks of beauty had caught something of which he was dimly conscious. Life had touched them with a vision, their hearts and souls were attuned to sweet harmonies of which the common world knew nothing."

Dreiser's Cowperwood was as driven by his passion to possess beautiful women as decorative and sexual objects as he was driven by his need for business triumph and his love of art. In that regard, he was typical of the powerful men (though more promiscuous than others and less sensitive than most) depicted in the classic literature of wealth written by Henry James, Edith Wharton, and Kate Chopin.

Both Henry James and Edith Wharton were born into wealthy families and in their formative years developed understandings of the culture of wealth that could only come to intelligent and sensitive participant-observers. Both later wrote great numbers of short stories and novels that explored the lives of wealthy characters, almost all of whom lived in New York City, or in France, England, or Italy. Neither displayed much sustained interest in American life beyond the narrow strip of the country that extended along the Atlantic coast from Boston to New York. Wharton, however, did write two fine short novels focused on deprived rural lives in Massachusetts, *Ethan Frome* (1911) and *Summer* (1917), while James wrote *The American Scene* (1907), in which he recorded his mostly horrified reactions to the quality of American city life. Like many of their characters, both James and Wharton became permanent expatriates, James moving to England in 1875, when he was 32, and Wharton moving to France in 1914, when she was 52.

Several core issues were involved in the culture of the wealthy, according to James and Wharton. These core issues included distinctions made regarding family status and power, the role of kinship networks, the power of traditions, the manner by which the wealth of individuals and families had been achieved, evolving definitions of proper taste and behavior; as well as methods of dealing with interlopers from other social classes, the misbehavior of members of the class, and occasional rebels. Characters were often motivated by the need to preserve family status and purity from interlopers who belonged to other classes. In the fiction by James that has become standard, such as his novella *Daisy Miller: A Study* (1879), the failure of a young girl's family to properly nurture her, and her resulting misbehavior, are the main issues. In widely read fiction by Wharton, such as *The Age of Innocence* (1920) and short stories such as "Souls Belated" and "The Other Two," the roles and status of women and the nature of relationships between men and women are central.

In *Daisy Miller*, the young, beautiful Daisy, accompanied by her mother and younger brother, is on a European tour and staying in places occupied for the most part by Europeanized expatriate Americans who maintain a strict code of conduct. Daisy's family is presented as horrifyingly vulgar. Her father, Ezra B. Miller, is a rich businessman in the small factory city of Schenectady, NY. Her mother does not sleep much, suffers from a liver ailment and from dyspepsia (that is, indigestion caused by an unhealthy diet), and is "dreadfully nervous." The father and brother Randolph also suffer from dyspepsia. Randolph, a child of nine or ten, speaks in almost pure slang and has already absorbed the very American opinion that America is "the best" at everything. He is allowed to wander around, day and night. He has already lost all but seven of his teeth as a result of gum disease or his addiction to sugar. He is described as an "urchin" by the narrator, an odd word to use to describe an upper-class child because it denotes a child of the streets who has no family. But it is appropriate because, in fact, Randolph is a neglected child, a de facto urchin. His mother does no effective parenting, no nurturing.

Daisy is also a neglected child. Her mother has not taught her how to speak, how to dress, how to behave with restraint, or how to avoid giving pain to others. Somewhere, of course, she has learned to believe that her opinions matter, that she is the equal of more experienced and knowledge-able people, and that she should follow her inclinations and urges. Daisy's behavior horrifies most of the people with whom she comes into contact and causes a great deal of discussion. What is so bad about her behavior? One of the leading members of the expatriate American society in Rome, Mrs. Walker, succinctly summarizes the general view of her improprieties: Daisy has been doing "Everything that is not done here. Flirting with any man she could pick up; sitting in corners with mysterious Italians; dancing all the evening with the same partners; receiving visits at eleven o'clock at night. Her mother goes away when visitors come." To which her defender, Winterbourne, responds on this occasion, as he does at other times, with the explanation that "The poor girl's only fault is that she is very unculti-vated," that she has not received the requisite nurturing she should have received.

Winterbourne's judgment of Daisy was humane in comparison to Mrs. Walker's. But, through the device of clashing points of view that James often utilized, readers are invited to consider that Winterbourne is moti-vated by a largely sexual interest in Daisy. He would never say so, of course, because that would not be proper. But the narrator provides us with certain details about Winterbourne which might lead us toward that conclusion. We are told he is a student. But the only thing he studies in the story is Daisy's physical appearance, her face and body, and the narrator says that "He had a great relish for feminine beauty; he was addicted to observing and analyzing it," which introduces Winterbourne's close analysis of Daisy's face and, a few pages later, his comment that "she had the tournure [i.e., the figure and bearing] of a princess." We are also given a strong hint that he was carrying on a long-term affair with an older, foreign woman in Geneva. In the code language of the wealthy community of expatriates, the fact that she was foreign and older suggests that Winterbourne was a libertine. This image of him sharply contrasts, of course, with Daisy's image of him as quaint, old-fashioned, and stiff.

Two 1879 reviews of *Daisy Miller* indicate that Daisy was understood at the time mostly as a badly behaved young girl. A reviewer in *Scribner's Monthly* said that James had conveyed through her "the filial impiety of many American girls, their recklessness of advice and their positive disobedience of parents" as well as the "attractiveness of such girls, together with the astonishment and pain she inflicts on Europeans and more refined Americans by her unruliness and audacity." A reviewer in the *North American Review* wrote that "Daisy Miller is a beauty, and, without being exactly a fool, is ignorant and devoid of all mental tone or character. She dressed elegantly, has the 'tournure of a princess,' and is yet irredeemably vulgar in her talk and her conduct." This reviewer thought that she would become "the accepted type and her name the sobriquet in European journalism of the American young woman of the period."[3] That Daisy *did* in fact become an "accepted type" of American young womanhood seems evident from comments by "society" writers 20 and more years later. For example, in her column in *Harper's Bazaar*, Katherine DeForest remarked in 1889 that Daisy Miller still existed in Paris salons, while in 1904 Winfield Scott Moody claimed in the *Ladies Home Journal* that Daisy was the forerunner of the contemporary ideal of the liberated woman, the iconic Gibson Girl.[4] In 1907, writing a comparison of American and British women in the *Youth's Companion*, Lady Henry Somerset concurred that Daisy represented the beginnings of profound changes in the nature of American womanhood. She also said that "the American woman has always seemed to me a sort of human automobile. Prolonged rest is ruin to a motor-car, and prolonged rest seems impossible to her. Change is her choice, and haste her progress; the one unendurable horror is monotony."[5]

Beautiful and wealthy young women in the fiction of Edith Wharton are, like Daisy, viewed by their men and often by other women as decorative and aesthetically pleasing objects who confer high social status and power on their owners. Near the beginning of *The Age of Innocence* (1920),

[3] "Henry James's 'Daisy Miller'," *Scribner's Monthly*, 17 (February 1879), p. 609; Richard Grant White, "Trollope's *Is he Popinjoy? James's The Europeans; James's Daisy Miller ...* ," *North American Review*, 128 (January/June 1879), pp. 97–108.
[4] Katharine DeForest, "Our Paris Letter," *Harper's Bazaar*, 32 (February 11, 1899), p. 111; Winfield Scott Moody, "Daisy Miller and the Gibson Girl," *Ladies Home Journal*, 21 (September 1904), p. 17.
[5] Lady Henry Somerset, "American and English Women," *Youth's Companion*, 81 (February 7, 1907), pp. 63–4.

for instance, Wharton describes the appearance of May Welland, the fiancée of Newland Archer, during a New York opera. May is dressed in white and, moved by the music, "a warm pink mounted to the girl's cheek, mantled her brow to the roots of her fair braids and suffused the young slope of her breast to the line where it met a modest tulle tucker with a single gardenia." As if she was a statue or a painting or a piece of furniture, Newland feels the "thrill of possessorship" of May. Similar scenes with similar thrills of possession or burning desires for possession occur often in Wharton's work. Sometimes, but not too often, the possessor grows during the novel and actually grants some degree of humanity to the object. Thus by the end of *The Age of Innocence* Newland shows some deeper understanding of May even though "he had long given up trying to disengage her real self from the shape into which tradition and training had moulded her."

Wharton understood more than any other American writer how wealth was expressed by the wealthy. At the beginning of her career, she coauthored a trend-setting book on high-style interior decoration and wrote books describing and assessing French and Italian gardens and landscapes. In her fiction, using an interior designer's or landscape architect's understanding of how built environments express deep truths about their designers and owners, she was adept at portraying characters by describing the sorts of homes and rooms they occupied. The highly conformist, narrow, and traditional Archer women of *The Age of Innocence* reside in an "an unclouded harmony of tastes and interests" among "cultivated ferns in Wardian cases, [they] made macramé lace and wool embroidery on linen, [and] collected American Revolutionary glazed ware. …" The home of the powerful Beaufort family, a major force in New York society, contained a ballroom that people entered "down a vista of enfiladed drawing rooms (the sea-green, the crimson, and the *bouton d'or*) seeing from afar the many-candled lustres reflected in the polished parquetry, and beyond that the depths of a conservatory where camellias and tree ferns arched their costly foliage over seats of black and gold bamboo." Ellen Olenska's drawing room in her house in the "Bohemian quarter" of New York, on the other hand, perfectly projects her mysterious, Europeanized, nonconforming character to Newland Archer: its few chairs and tables were grouped in an unusual way, a vase held only two roses instead of the usual dozen, and there was "a vague pervading perfume that was not what one put on handkerchiefs, but rather like the scent of some far-off bazaar, a smell made up of Turkish coffee and ambergris and dried roses."

Built on layers of detail about dress, posture, gardens, rooms, hairdos, skin pigmentation and texture, architecture, interior plants, paintings, contemporary French and British literature, music, opera, and so forth, many of Wharton's characterizations of wealthy people present difficulties to modern readers. We can figure her meanings through context, but we simply do not know very much about the consumer goods and art she puts on display. But the rebellion of some of her women from being possessed is perfectly clear. Such rebellious women, contrasted to women characters such as May who willingly serve as owned objects, are among her most impressive and attractive creations who, for readers of the time, may have been fictional representatives of the many prominent women who accomplished much without marriage or after divorce. Ellen Olenska was probably the most impressive of these women, both because she refused continued imprisonment by her European husband and because she refused Newland Archer. Another is Lydia Tillotson in the 1899 story "Souls Belated"; Lydia, who is undergoing a divorce, brilliantly and accurately analyzes the "hundred ties of pity and self-reproach" that bind her lover to her, decides for independence and liberty, and moves on.

The most extended turn-of-the-twentieth-century exploration of the effects of marital estrangement on a wealthy woman was, I think, Kate Chopin's novel *The Awakening* (1899). Chopin was as blunt as Wharton in her description of how Edna Pontellier's husband views her as an object, a commodity, describing him at the beginning of her novel as "looking at his wife as one looks at a valuable piece of property which has suffered some damage." The damage involved here is the sunburn that Edna has acquired on a Gulf of Mexico beach south of the family's home city of New Orleans.

The Awakening brilliantly depicts upper-class New Orleans French Creole society. To emphasize the artfulness (and artificiality) of that society, it uses pictorial images that often read like Impressionist and other contemporary painting that adorned the homes of the wealthy. Just before she remarked about Mr. Pontellier's property interest in Edna, Chopin has him look out over a vivid, beautifully composed landscape:

> He fixed his eyes upon a white sunshade that was advancing at snail's pace from the beach. He could see it plainly between the gaunt trunks of the water-oaks and across the stretch of yellow chamomile. The gulf looked far away, melting hazily into the blue of the horizon. The sunshade continued to approach slowly. Beneath its pink-lined shelter were his wife, Mrs. Pontellier, and young Robert Lebrun.

Later in the novel, we are given a number of painterly interiors, table settings, and still lifes. A garden café is described as "a small, leafy corner, with a few green tables under the orange trees"; shortly after this description, one of the green tables is described as "blotched with the checkered sunlight that filtered through the quivering leaves overhead." A dinner party table is described as "gorgeous," with "an effect of splendor conveyed by a cover of pale yellow satin under strips of lace-work. There were wax candles in massive brass candelabra, burning softly under yellow silk shades; full fragrant roses, yellow and red, abounded. There were silver and gold … and crystal which glittered like the gems which the women wore." She describes "gold and silver cake arranged on platters in alternate slices." A box of sweets is described as full of "luscious and toothsome bits – the finest of fruits, pates, a rare bottle or two, delicious syrups, and bonbons in abundance." Late in the novel, Edna moves out of her husband's beautiful, sumptuous house to take up residence in a small unpretentious house with a neglected garden. How she decorates her parlor suggests much about her desire for a simpler life: "There were some books on the table and a lounge near at hand. On the floor was a fresh matting, covered with a rug or two; and on the walls hung a few tasteful pictures."

Chopin, like her contemporary Edith Wharton, provides her readers carefully textured scenes in which wealth and good taste is displayed. She also provides a series of portraits depicting Edna Pontellier that, as they accumulate, serve as pictorial analogues to her stages of rebellion from social conventions, her estrangement from her suffocating husband, and her awakening identity. An early portrait reads:

> Mrs. Pontellier's eyes were quick and bright; they were a yellowish brown, about the color of her hair. She had a way of turning them swiftly upon an object and holding them there as if lost in some inward maze of contemplation or thought. Her eyebrows were a shade darker than her hair. They were thick and almost horizontal, emphasizing the depth of her eyes. She was rather handsome than beautiful. Her face was captivating by reason of a certain frankness of expression and a contradictory subtle play of features. Her manner was engaging.

Later, we are given pictures such as the one in which we are told that the lines of her body are "long, clean and symmetrical; it was a body which fell into splendid poses; there was no suggestion of the trim, stereotyped fashion-plate about it." Still later, we are given an image of her in evening clothes: "The golden shimmer of Edna's satin gown spread its rich folds on either side of her. There was a soft fall of lace encircling her shoulders. It was the color of her skin, without the glow, the myriad living tints that one may sometimes discover in vibrant flesh." At the end of the novel, she appears as a primordial nude:

> But when she was there beside the sea, absolutely alone, she cast the unpleasant, pricking garments from her, and for the first time in her life she stood naked in the open air, at the mercy of the sun, the breeze that beat upon her, and the waves that invited her. How strange and awful it seemed to stand naked under the sky! how delicious! She felt like some new born creature, opening its eyes in a familiar world that it had never known. The foamy wavelets curled up to her white feet, and coiled like serpents around her ankles.

One of the main features of the classic fiction of wealth that I have been discussing is that, except for their contact with servants and with occasional interlopers, wealthy characters, unless in a state of utter rebellion like Ellen Olenska or Edna Pontellier, have no contact with people of other classes. They live entirely in a sumptuous rich world, knowing nothing of the people surrounding them. In that regard, they are exact duplicates of the characters in the classic literature of poverty and exact representations of the hugely separate and unequal worlds in which Americans of the era lived their lives.

6

To Change America

Stunning US accomplishments of the late nineteenth and early twentieth centuries – technological breakthroughs, engineering marvels, business advances, astonishing accumulations of wealth, world leadership in the production of some commodities, and so forth – were regularly celebrated in newspaper and magazine articles, biographies and autobiographies, speeches, world's fairs, and expositions. But the country, even from the points of view of some of its most intelligent, accomplished, and celebrated public figures, was beset by massive poverty and inequality, economic boom periods followed by harsh depressions, social tensions manifested in riots and "massacres," and a general sense of profound instability. Those negative qualities gave rise to a great number of reform and revolutionary movements. The most serious among them were the Temperance movement, the union movement, and the various socialist movements.

Temperance

The context

The largest, longest, and, arguably, the most successful social change movement of nineteenth- and early twentieth-century America was the Temperance movement, which claimed that alcohol use was the primary cause of individual failure, family dysfunction, and social unrest. Loosely allied to similar movements in Britain, in the Scandinavian countries, and in many other parts of the world, the American Temperance movement started in the late eighteenth century, spread and became increasingly powerful in the 1830s, began in the 1850s to get antialcohol legislation passed by some local and state governments, became a major force in national politics after the Civil War, and achieved its national goal in 1920. In that year, the Eighteenth Amendment to the Constitution, which prohibited the manufacture or distribution of alcohol, went into effect (it was repealed in 1933). Alcohol use was also prohibited or sharply curtailed in several other countries during the same period. Beginning in 1900, parts of Canada became "dry"; between 1914 and 1919 national prohibition or alcohol rationing laws were passed in Russia, Sweden, Iceland, Norway, Hungary, and Finland.

The American version of the Temperance movement was part of the general effort to develop clean, regular, wholesome ways of living as alternatives to the perceived unwholesome, chaotic, self-destructive ways of society. The liquids and foods people put into their bodies were subjects of mounting concern in the nineteenth century. Growing problems of water contamination in industrialized areas led to efforts to discover ways to purify contaminated water, to discover new sources of pure water, and to find ways to pipe pure water from the countryside into population centers. By the end of the century, the low quality of meat produced by large, industrialized packinghouses, and the sale of contaminated products, were causes of widespread alarm. Ultimately, public health laws brought some measure of regulation to the industry. For some Americans, however, vegetarianism was the obvious alternative to consumption of either regulated or unregulated meat. By 1900, some grain-based foods that were said to have very positive effects on health were being sold. The most widely known of these were Graham Crackers, Grape Nuts, and shredded wheat.

Alcohol consumption was a greater national concern than water and food consumption. Though there were occasional quick deaths by poisoning, bad water and bad meat usually affected people over years. But the effects of alcohol consumption, according to Temperance advocates, were immediate and severe. A drink could lead to a poor decision that could reverberate for years. Men and boys, who were widely believed to be prone "by nature" to act on irrational, passionate impulses, lost all self-control after a few drinks – their tempers flared, they fought, they maimed and killed each other. Men spent their pay in saloons and became so addicted to drink that they could not or would not work. Their families were thus driven down into poverty. Drinking men beat their wives and abused their children. Women drank, too, because, it was said, they were without hope and because they wished to escape from their abusive men.

Any social change movement, especially one that lasted more than a hundred years, needs an understandable analysis of the problem it is trying to address, a clear goal, and the ability to have its message heard and believed. By any measure, the Temperance movement possessed all these necessities. It clearly described the ineluctable downward spiral caused by drinking. Its evidence was observable and transparent: saloons were everywhere, and it was easy for anyone to see that people who drank became, to one degree or another, something other than who they were. Beyond the clarity of its description and the power of its evidence, the Temperance movement also had clear goals, an unwavering conviction that its aims and methods were proper and just, a leadership that was, usually, mutually supportive, an ability to pass on its ideas to new generations of believers, and a set of messages that were widely disseminated through the written and spoken word.

After the Civil War, the movement was spearheaded by the Women's Christian Temperance Union. The WCTU was founded in 1874, a few months after the beginning in Ohio of women's "crusades" against alcohol that included prayer meetings outside saloons that were aimed at convincing drinkers to stop drinking and saloon owners to close their doors forever. Over the ensuing decades, the WCTU broadened its agenda to include suffrage (that is, equal voting rights for women), prison reform, the reform of state laws that permitted marriage at age 12 for girls and age 14 for boys, the passage of laws regulating food and drug manufacture and distribution, sex education, and Temperance education in the schools. But its primary goals were convincing Americans of the evil effects of alcohol and, ultimately, achieving universal prohibition.

The literature

Temperance was the most written about and most spoken about social change issue of the nineteenth century. It was the cause and subject of an immense popular literature and the subject of millions of speeches and sermons. Narratives about the recoveries of people who stopped drinking and were "born again" were among the staples of inspirational literature.

In 1913, Jack London, the most famous American author of the time, published *John Barleycorn* first as a serial in the widely popular *Saturday Evening Post* and then as a book. The closest thing to an autobiography he ever wrote, the book detailed London's lifetime of drinking as a worker, as a man who enjoyed saloons, and as a binge drinker. Over the next several years, *John Barleycorn* was utilized by Temperance movement speakers and writers as compelling testimony.

No other American writer served the Temperance cause so directly as London. But many shared the Temperance belief that alcohol was the primary cause of bad decisions, self-destructive behavior, violence directed at others, and so forth. In many pre-1920 classics, including some that I have already mentioned or discussed, drinking was pivotal and decisive in terms of how it shaped character.

Drinking is a central issue in Twain's *Huckleberry Finn*. Pap Finn, Huck's father, is known as a man who "used to lay drunk with the hogs in the tanyard," who beat his son when he was sober, who got drunk every time he got money, and who on one occasion measures how much whiskey he has by saying he has enough for "two drunks and one delirium tremens." Drinking is also the catalyst for the expression of the general stupidity, crassness, and violence of Twain's ordinary folk. Whiskey is being drunk as his two friends debate whether to kill Jim Turner in the chapter titled "Better Let Blame Well Alone." In "An Arkansas Difficulty," families drink and fight on market day in the town, after which the wildly drunken Boggs is murdered by Colonel Sherburn. The Duke and the King often turn to their bottles, as at the end of "The Gold Saves the Thieves." They also give Temperance lectures from which, however, "they didn't make enough for them both to get drunk on." Twain's dubiousness about reformed drinkers is conveyed when Pap is talked out of his drinking by the Judge and his wife and, after talk about this being "the holiest time on record" and lots of tears, signs a pledge to never drink again. Pap's reform lasts only into his first alcohol-free night, when he sneaks out of the Judge's house, trades the new coat he has been given for a jug of whiskey, and gets "drunk as a fiddler."

Drinking is the immediate cause of extreme social and family dysfunction in Stephen Crane's *Maggie: A Girl of the Streets* (1893). Maggie is the daughter of a constantly drunken, violent mother and father; her brother seems to be following in the footsteps of the parents; and her boyfriend, a bartender by trade, also drinks heavily. New York saloons call "seductively" to people "to enter and annihilate sorrow or create rage." Uneducated and inarticulate to begin with, and given to self-delusional notions about their strengths and accomplishments, Crane's working-class characters further confuse themselves and then destroy themselves by drinking. The same behaviors occur in other Crane fictions. For instance, in the often reprinted story "The Blue Hotel," whiskey is the source of the erratic behavior that causes the Swede's death in a Nebraska saloon, while in the comic "The Bride Comes to Yellow Sky," a Texas story, Scratchy Wilson's "face flamed in a rage begot of whisky" when he challenges the local sheriff to fight.

Crane's parents were Temperance movement people and he certainly understood the usual arguments about drink as the cause of social disorder. But, like Twain before him, he was most interested in examining the behavior of drinkers, not speculating on the causes of their addiction. Causation, especially the social and economic conditions that allegedly led working people to drink, is a primary interest of Upton Sinclair in *The Jungle* (1906). Working people, Sinclair argues, drink because capitalism destroys their minds and bodies (Sinclair was not just theorizing for his novel, he was a lifelong practitioner of "total abstinence"). Less than two years after he came to the US from Lithuania, Jurgis Rudkus, Sinclair's protagonist, had been reduced to working in the "steaming pit of hell" of a fertilizer plant and realized that now "there was not an organ of his body that did its work without pain." Then he discovered that through drink he "could forget the pain, he could slip off the burden" and be a man again, feel good again. Before long, the craving for drink filled every one of his conscious moments. When he can find work, he drinks his pay. On the road in the farmlands, he tramps with many other men "until the hunger for drink and for women mastered them, and then went to work with a purpose in mind, and stopped when they had the price of a spree" including "wild rioting and debauchery" with prostitutes. Similarly, black workers, used to replace white workers during a strike, are given whiskey and women so that "there were stabbings and shootings, rape and murder stalking abroad."

Jurgis discovers drink in Chapter 14 of *The Jungle* and he continues drinking himself blind, except when he is in jail, until Chapter 32, when he stumbles upon a socialist meeting and is "converted," saved by the socialist analysis of how capitalism destroys people, and given hope for the future. *The Jungle* is often said (by people who have not completely read it) to be an exposé of the meatpacking industry, and there are in fact many extended passages in several of its 36 chapters about that industry's grotesque and disgusting manufacturing practices. But its main character and many of his fellows suffer mostly from bad jobs and alcohol addiction, not from contaminated meat.

Alcohol is also often disastrously involved at crucial moments in turn-of-the-century narratives about substantial men and women. In Frank Norris's *McTeague* (1899), alcohol addiction and behavioral dysfunction is passed from father to son. In Willa Cather's *O Pioneers!* the death of Emil and Marie was triggered by Frank Shabata's drinking. Many other iconic novels and stories use drink as the triggering device for life-changing events. Theodore Dreiser's George Hurstwood in *Sister Carrie* (1900) is the well-paid, married, nearly 40-year-old manager of Fitzgerald and Moy's "resort," or upper-class saloon, in downtown Chicago. He drinks only rarely and then only among "notabilities," men of "known ability." On one such occasion, during a period in his life when he is struggling with his desire for the 17-year-old Carrie, Hurstwood drinks too much. His mind becomes "warm in its fancies" as he considers whether to steal money from his employer's safe: "Wine was in his veins. It had crept up into his head and given him a warm view of the situation. It also colored the possibilities of ten thousand [dollars] for him. He could get Carrie. Oh, yes, he could! He could get rid of his wife." Trembling between "duty and desire," "flushed with the fumes of liquor," he has the money in his hand when, apparently by accident, the safe door closes. Did he, then, take the money inadvertently? Dreiser leaves that as an interesting, complicating question. But there was no question that at this crucial moment in the novel, a moment which begins the fall of Hurstwood and the rise of Carrie, drink is involved.

The Union Movement

In typical American workplaces, employers unilaterally decided the amount of an employee's wages, the number of hours to be worked in a day, the number of days to be worked in a week, the conditions under which the work was to be done, whether the employee would continue to work or be terminated, and whether the termination would occur with or without advanced notice. If the employee did not like the conditions set by the employer, he or she could quit and seek work elsewhere.

Unions sought to bring together workers for the purpose of negotiating wages and working conditions with employers. This negotiation could be done by the workers themselves or the workers could ask an outside organization with special expertise and resources to negotiate for them. The concept of negotiation was itself a profound challenge to employer power. It was therefore sharply resisted.

Employers sometimes resisted unions through the courts and through the legislative system. A complex and interesting legal and legislative history arose from this form of resistance. But it was the raw and dramatic

confrontation of workers and employers in strikes and other actions that
caught the public's attention (and, at certain moments, the attention of a
great number of writers).

Conflicts between employers and employees typically went through
several stages: (1) the employees asked the employers to negotiate wages
and working conditions with them or with their union; (2) the employers
refused; (3) the employees used the chief weapon at their disposal, the
strike, closing down the employers' operations and causing them economic
losses (alternatively, the employers preempted the employees by locking
them out when strikes loomed); and (4) the employers could then decide
whether to negotiate or to continue resisting. If the employers decided to
continue resisting, they had several tactics at their disposal. They could
"take the strike," absorb their own economic losses but let the strike go on
until the strikers gave up. If the strikers did not give up, employers could
hire replacement workers ("scabs" in the language of strikers) and also hire
men to fight the strikers, who would attempt to stop the scabs from
working. The niceties of the law were not involved in these tactics. Force
and toughness and the ability to do violence were all that mattered, for
both sides.

Large businesses often employed private police forces to do battle. If
they were overwhelmed, though, the employers could get the local authorities to assign the police to protect their property and otherwise control the
strikers. If that did not work and the strike was large enough to command
attention from politicians, the employers could ask the state governor to
support them by sending in state-operated militia troops to protect their
property. In some more extreme situations, martial law was declared,
which usually meant the imposition of a curfew, the suspension of constitutional guarantees regarding the First Amendment right to speak and
to gather in groups, and the suspension of the writ of *habeas corpus*.
Extreme situations were not rare. According to one "conservative" esti-
mate, between 1870 and 1900 at least 150 strikes and lockouts led to militia
mobilizations.

Manufacturing, railroad, and mining strikes occurred with great frequency in turn-of-the-twentieth-century America. But there was significant ebb and flow. According to the Federal Bureau of Labor Statistics,
there were 477 strikes involving 130,000 workers in 1881, which more
than tripled to 1,572 involving 610,000 workers in 1886, which more than
doubled to 3,648 involving 788,000 workers in 1903. The 1903 numbers
meant that 8.4 percent of the American workforce was out on strike for

some time during that year. Strike activity ebbed for several years. Then, what contemporaries referred to as "strike fever" broke out between 1915 and 1920. There were 3,789 strikes involving 1,660,000 workers in 1916, there were 4,450 involving 1,227,000 workers in 1917, there were 3,353 involving 1,240,000 workers in 1918, and 3,630 involving 4,160,000 workers in 1919. The 1919 numbers, which broke all records, meant that about 20 percent of the American workforce was out on strike sometime that year.

With few exceptions, mainstream newspaper and magazine coverage of labor news in general and strikes in particular favored employers. Some major strikes were barely mentioned by mass magazines and top dailies such as the *New York Times*. When strike reporting did occur, a good deal of it characterized employers as pillars of the community, while strikers were characterized as ignorant, drunken, crazed immigrant "rioters." This conflation of strikes with immigrants was not without cause. Immigrants were deeply involved in strikes. That was because they held a significant number of the dirty, difficult, dangerous, and poorly paid jobs in precisely those industries, mostly located in major cities, where the demands for unionization were most insistent. This involvement with unions led to the further stereotyping of immigrant workers as people who "bit the hand that fed them" and to the stereotyping of the labor movement in general as dominated by city "foreigners."

Faced with a largely hostile mainstream press, the union movement and its sympathizers developed hundreds of magazines and newspapers in which the heroic efforts of workers were celebrated and the bad behavior of employers, politicians, scabs, the police, and the military was bitterly denounced. Full of action and violence, martyrdom and heroism, good people and bad people, fighters for freedom and oppressors, stories of strikes became one of the chief ways of expressing the experience of the exploited worker. None of the most often told strike stories involved clear, decisive, long-term victories for workers. Rather, they illustrated the union understanding of the core characteristics and modes of behavior of employees, employers, and representatives of government. Several were told so often that they became mythological. What follows here are brief summaries of some of these:

• In June 1877, during the depression that had begun in 1873, employees of some of the large railroads protested when their wages were cut. The protests began in West Virginia, spread north, then west, and within a few days virtually all rail traffic east of the Mississippi River was stopped.

Other workers left their jobs in support of the railroad workers or because of their own grievances; Saint Louis underwent a general strike of virtually all workers. Strikers were most effective in Pennsylvania because they were joined by coal miners, who were angry about the recent executions of several "Molly McGuire" Irish miners for alleged attempts to subvert the state. Ultimately, after a month of battles and failed efforts to restore order, some 2,700 US Army troops were deployed to reopen the railroads at bayonet point.

• The Haymarket "affair" of May 1886 developed out of widespread Chicago demonstrations in favor of an eight-hour workday (the workday was then 10 to 12 hours) and a particular strike during which the police, allegedly unprovoked, fired into a crowd of strikers. One of the protests against that action was held in the city's Haymarket Square. The meeting was entirely peaceful, even according to the Mayor of Chicago, who attended. During one of the last speeches, the police inexplicably marched in. A bomb was thrown, several policeman were killed and many more injured; in the melee that followed, there was further death and injury. The attack on the police provoked panic across the country, with many predicting that foreign "anarchists" were fomenting a revolution. The speakers in Haymarket Square were indeed anarchists. Eight of them were arrested and charged with conspiracy to murder the police. No evidence was introduced to link any of them to the bomb, and much of the most damaging trial testimony against them was later judged by the Governor of Illinois, following a long, detailed investigation, to have been perjurious. But all eight were convicted. Seven were sentenced to be executed, one was given a 15-year prison term. Two of the men had their sentences commuted to life in prison. One, Lewis Lingg, in an anarchist gesture against the power of the state, blew himself up on the eve of his execution with dynamite that had been smuggled into prison (though there were other versions of his end which claim that he was murdered). Four were hanged in November 1887.

• The 1892 strike at Andrew Carnegie's Homestead Steel Works in Homestead, Pennsylvania, began with a wage cut, which led to protests by several thousand workers, then to a lockout, then to a pitched battle between workers and Pinkerton detectives hired to defend the interest of the company, and finally to the imposition of martial law in Homestead by the Governor of Pennsylvania. The incipient steel workers union was broken in this strike, but so too, at least to some observers, was Carnegie's reputation as a beneficent person. Near the end of the strike, anarchist Alexander Berkman, who was then the lover of Emma Goldman, tried to murder Henry Clay Frick, who managed Homestead. He failed. Frick emerged as a stalwart hero. Berkman was sentenced to a long prison term.

- Probably the deepest of the nineteenth-century depressions began in 1893. The next year was chaotic. First, there was a coal miner strike centered in Ohio, Illinois, Pennsylvania, and West Virginia, where martial law declarations were widespread. Then there was the eviction of striking miners by the military from the Choctaw Nation of Indian Territory, dubbed by the *United Mine Workers Journal* as the "Siberia of America." Then in late spring there was the appearance in the far West of several "industrial armies" of unemployed men who took to the road in search of work (the most famous was Coxey's Army). Some "armies" stole railroad trains to move east, leading to the deployment of US Army units in the Southwest, California, Oregon, Montana, and the Dakotas. In this context, the American Railway Union, led by Eugene Debs, struck against the Pullman Palace Car Company of Illinois, manufacturer of Pullman railroad cars. That localized action grew exponentially when in June the union announced a boycott of any train on any US railroad that included a Pullman car. Before long, the union had closed down most of the country's rail system. The Federal government stepped in, got an injunction against the union, jailed Debs and other leaders, deployed Army forces to open the railroads, and ultimately restored order. During his months in jail, Debs said, he became a socialist. Several years later, he became the leader of the Socialist Party of America.

- A 1912 strike against textile factories in Lawrence, Massachusetts, began when owners cut weekly wages down from the standard $8.76 because the Massachusetts State Legislature had mandated that they reduce the work week from 56 to 54 hours. The strike – involving 20,000 workers from 30 different countries who spoke 45 different languages – lasted two months and led to the mobilization of the state militia and a great number of arrests.

- In February 1913, a strike began by some 25,000 mostly immigrant workers in Paterson, New Jersey, against 300 silk mills. This strike involved a great deal of collateral activity, including a "Pageant" reenactment of key events in Madison Square Garden in Manhattan while the strike was still underway. The strike ended after five months.

- In 1913, a statewide strike involving thousands of mine workers in Colorado against the Rockefeller family's Colorado Fuel and Iron Company broke out. For the twelfth time since 1894, martial law was declared in Colorado. A "massacre" occurred at the town of Ludlow, when troops fired into a crowd, killing or wounding several dozen men, women, and children.

There were, of course, management versions of the same strikes and lockouts. These stressed the existence of benevolent employers beset by market forces, union leaders motivated by a wish for power, ignorant and simple-minded workers misled into riotous violence, communities crying out for the restoration of law and order, and the police and military as agents of peace.

Every union seeking regional or national power struggled with the core issue of what kinds of workers were to be represented, precisely who would be admitted as members. One of the later nineteenth-century unions which developed some power, the Knights of Labor, for example, struggled over race and gender issues: it supported the Chinese Exclusion Act of 1882, but in 1883 it made great strides toward inclusiveness when it opened its ranks to women and blacks (and employers, too, strangely enough). Founded in 1886, the American Federation of Labor (AFL), defined itself by admitting only skilled workers such as people in the building trades and in the traditional crafts (that is why the AFL referred to itself as a craft union or trade union). But, in effect, this was also a racial, ethnic, and gender definition, since nearly all such skilled jobs were held by white men. Founded in Chicago 1905, the Industrial Workers of the World, or IWW (the members of which were called "Wobblies"), defined itself by its inclusiveness. It existed for any "wage slave," as it called a person beholden to another for his or her "living," regardless of race, gender, or ethnicity. In contrast to the AFL, which it accused of existing only for "aristocratic" skilled workers, it sought to unionize unskilled and semiskilled workers such as factory workers and farm laborers across whole industries (hence, it was an "industrial" union).

The IWW was sometimes described as an "anarcho-syndicalist" organization, that is, a union (a "syndicate," in European terms) that also had an anarchist orientation. Anarchism was based on the belief that all governments were coercive and acted by force. Governments should therefore, according to anarchists, be abolished, leaving the people to govern themselves. Left to themselves, without government, men and women would devise ways to live harmoniously, to respect individual opinion, to avoid all uses of force and coercion. Founded on extreme belief in the sanctity and goodness of individuals, anarchism thus sought extreme democratization and extremely decentralized decision making.

European anarchists in the late nineteenth century stressed the "propaganda of the deed" to achieve the abolition of government. The greatest potential deed was the murder of a head of state, after which the working class would rise up in revolt. American anarchists sometimes expressed that same belief and occasionally acted on it, as when the anarchist Alexander Berkman attempted to murder Henry Clay Frick during the Homestead Strike. Many, though, describing themselves as "philosophical" anarchists, renounced violence (though not always consistently) and emphasized that worker liberation was to begin in the individual consciousness and individual efforts to free themselves. Emma Goldman was the most influential of the philosophical anarchists. Goldman often stressed the roles of art and literature and sexual liberation in the revolution she thought was underway. Anarchist antistate beliefs and a belief in galvanizing strikes and apocalyptic general strikes (that is, strikes by the entire workforce) infused IWW rhetoric.

IWW inclusiveness as opposed to AFL exclusiveness was one of the key differences between the two unions. A second difference had to do with overall goals. The AFL believed in what its leader, Samuel Gompers, called "unionism pure and simple," which meant the business of negotiating contracts with employers that gave its members better wages and working conditions. It did not wish to become involved in political or social reform movements. In contrast, the IWW had the overall goal of "abolishing" wage slavery, thus seeing itself as a sort of second stage of the Abolition movement which had sought to free chattel slaves. It sought, as it loudly and constantly proclaimed, to foment a revolution that would "build the new society in the shell of the old." It would achieve its revolution through "direct action" in the streets, through constant agitation, through sabotage, and through strikes that would ultimately lead to a "general strike" of all workers. Furthermore, it refused to sign contracts with capitalists. It advised its members to settle issues verbally and to return to work but only until they were strong enough to strike again. The real end of the virtually perpetual strike would come when a vast general strike would destroy the capitalist economy.

Its enemies often called it an "Impossibilist" organization and said the initials IWW stood for "I Won't Work" or "I Want Whiskey." Whatever its real world possibilities, in its heyday, the decade or so before 1917, it received a great deal of attention in the nation's press. Its national spokespeople were charismatic. Its leader, "Big Bill" Haywood, was a giant of a man who was born in the far West and spent his early career as a miner, looked and sounded tough as nails, but on occasion seemed sensitive, almost sweet. Elizabeth Gurley Flynn, called a fearless "rebel girl," was a fantastic speaker who seemed to live off crowds.

The IWW was very adept at communicating its messages. It utilized plain style prose to lay out its critique and its program, and it also used street speakers and lecturers. But it mostly depended on funny, stirring, catchy songs that could be learned "by heart" by its largely uneducated members. Poets and song writers like Joe Hill, Ralph Chaplin, and T-Bone Slim were gifted lyricists who sometimes utilized melodies that were already known to their audiences. (IWW writers were not the first to set new words to old melodies – Temperance songwriters had long used the device.)

Ralph Chaplin had the distinction of writing the poem, quickly set to music, that would become not just an IWW mainstay but also "labor's national anthem." On January 9, 1915, "Solidarity Forever" was published in the IWW weekly newspaper. It was written to the tune familiar to every schoolchild, "The Battle Hymn of the Republic" (the same tune as "John Brown's Body"), with the refrain of "Glory, glory, hallelujah / His truth goes marching on" changed to "Solidarity forever / For the union makes us strong." In several sharp stanzas, it laid out IWW beliefs about the "feeble strength" of the individual and the potential power of the union, the irreconcilable differences between "the greedy parasite" and the workers who produced everything, the injustice of the ownership of everything by "idle drones," and the glorious future in which revolutionary workers would "bring to birth the new world from the ashes of the old." That is, in several quick stanzas, "Solidarity Forever" managed to summarize a lot, if not all that a revolutionary needed to know. And it did all this in a melody that demanded passion from individual singers and that could be awesome when sung by a large group.

Joe Hill, known as the "Wobbly Bard," authored such labor standbys as "The Preacher and the Slave," "Casey Jones – The Union Scab," "Mr. Block," and "There is Power in a Union." He could probably have become rich by using his talent to write commercial sheet music, but he continued working as a manual laborer despite his considerable fame. His death, though, was what cemented his reputation. In 1914, Hill had been arrested for the murder of a grocery store owner in Salt Lake City, Utah, during a holdup. What many, and not just other Wobblies, saw as weak evidence was used against him, but he was convicted in June, 1915. There were significant efforts made at the national level to get the Governor of Utah to order a new trial. Demonstrations were held. An appeal to the Governor was made by President Wilson. Helen Keller, who was active in radical circles, became involved, as did Samuel Gompers of the IWW's arch-rival AFL. All of these appeals fell on deaf ears. Hill was executed by firing squad on November 19, 1915 (careful readers will note that this was about one week before the first cross burning by the new KKK at Stone Mountain, Georgia).

Hill's death quickly became another cautionary story about the plight of workers in the United States, the fierce opposition of capitalist monsters, who allegedly engineered his execution, and the need for a revolutionary union. Hill apparently died with great dignity and some humor, writing a telegram to Bill Haywood just before his execution that said, "Goodbye Bill: I die like a true rebel. Don't waste any time mourning – organize! It is a hundred miles from here to Wyoming. Could you arrange to have my body hauled to the state line to be buried. I don't want to be found dead in Utah." A while later Hill was given an extravaganza of a funeral in Chicago, the international headquarters of the IWW. His songs were sung before the orators spoke. His casket was carried several miles through the streets in a huge parade. Newspaper photos showed that the streets were lined by spectators. Ralph Chaplin reported the scene for the Chicago-based *International Socialist Review*: "Songs were sung all along the way, chiefly Joe Hill's, although some of the foreign-speaking workers sang revolutionary songs in their own native tongues. As soon as a song would die down in one place, the same song or another would be taken up by other voices along the line."

Socialisms

The context

To most of its nineteenth-century adherents, socialism meant concern for society in general as opposed to concern for purely personal things. Americans who called themselves socialists subscribed to the same general propositions as European socialists: that ordinary people were victimized by profit-hungry individuals and corporations and that a new era of social cooperation and fairness could be achieved. They believed that a socialist society would be one in which the community owned and administered in the interest of all its members the major property (e.g., land, transportation systems, factories, mines, and so forth) that was currently privately owned and administered in the interest of an individual or a small group of investors.

In its first stages, beginning in the late eighteenth century, American socialism was practiced in hundreds of small communities established as model societies that could, in theory, be imitated and expanded to serve larger numbers of people. Many of the most successful of these small communities were Christian in origin and were attempting, according to their leaders, to reproduce heaven on earth or to prepare the way for the Second Coming. They were usually called "biblical communist" or "biblical socialist" societies. Their premises, typically, were that all human beings were of equal worth, that private property separated individuals from each other, and that shared wealth and cooperation created a positive environment in which new kinds of loving human relationships and intense religious devotion could flourish.

Some of the communities became famous not just because of their ideas or because of the particular forms of their Christianity but because they were highly productive, because they created new workplace arrangements, and because they developed interesting kinds of relationships among their members. Shaker communities, for instance, were very successful producers of commercial garden and farm seeds for much of the nineteenth century; they produced beautifully designed furniture; they managed to substantially reduce the workday and workweek for members; and they taught multiple skills to members so that, in a given month, a person could rotate through several jobs, thereby avoiding the usual tedium of work. The Oneida community, while producing high quality small game traps and tableware, was most interesting for its practice of "multiple marriage" (i.e., members were expected to have several "amative" partners in any given period of time), its practice of male sexual "continence" (*coitus reservatus*), its attempt to improve individual behavior through organized "mutual criticism," its practice of selective breeding of people, and its practice of community child rearing.

Prior to and after the Civil War, many of the communities, including the Shakers and Oneidans, invited visits from the public in order to spread their news about the new human possibilities they claimed to have discovered. Charles Nordhoff, who over a few years visited and studied some

72 different communities with a combined population of about 5,000, wrote a detailed account of many of them in *The Communistic Societies of the United States* (1875). A tough-minded and skeptical observer, Nordhoff nonetheless concluded that community ownership of property and social-mindedness had produced, in many instances, very successful societies. He said that the communities enjoyed "a greater amount of comfort, and vastly greater security against want and demoralization, than were attained by their neighbors or the surrounding population, with better schools and opportunities for training for their children, and far less exposure for the women, the aged and infirm." He praised the strength of communist families, their good health, their temperance, their cleanliness, the quality of their food, and their longevity. He was particularly interested in how women fared in the communities. Communist women, he said, lived "without exception, I think, far less burdensome lives than women of the same class elsewhere." He explained that there were two causes for this positive result. First, men lived regular lives and did not spend time drinking in saloons and other "places of dissipation." Second, everything in the communist societies was so "systematized and regular" that women were relieved of various chores while their men provided them conveniences that "the migratory farmer's wife sighs for in vain."[1] Nordhoff's conclusions about the better ways of living that he studied were published in the middle of a deep economic depression marked by a great deal of conflict, and this no doubt sharpened their impact on readers.

A second stage in the history of American socialism began to develop after the publication of Edward Bellamy's utopian novel, *Looking Backward* (1887). To describe his imagined ideal society, Bellamy used the ploy of having his protagonist go to sleep in 1887, sleep through a fire that destroyed his house except for his fireproof bedroom, and wake up from his state of "suspended animation" in the year 2000 to discover that divisiveness, conflict, and violence no longer existed. Structured according to the precepts of "Nationalism," Bellamy's substitute word for "socialism," the world was now entirely orderly, rational, classless, cooperative, technologically advanced, educated, civilized, and genteel. How had this amazing world come about? It came about because people had realized that the irrational behaviors of the late nineteenth century were destructive and had then decided to behave rationally.

---

[1]   Nordhoff text is available at: //sacred-texts.com/utopia/csus/csus30.htm

Bellamy's book was so influential that for a few years Nationalist "clubs" tried to promote the beginnings of the new epoch. But its real contribution, I think, was that it popularized two related propositions that American socialists of a certain type would continue to utilize. One was the proposition that fundamental social change could be achieved through the exercise of human reason. The second was that, once reason prevailed, there were no limits to what human beings could accomplish together. Socialists who believed in these propositions soon developed an understanding, they said, of how they could bring about fundamental social change through an orderly, logical step-by-step process. First, the masses would be taught that socialism was in their interest. Second, the educated masses would elect socialists to municipal, state, and national offices. Third, these elected leaders, supported by their socialist constituents, would pass new laws that would create better economic and social conditions and also demonstrate the good that could be done by clean, efficient government. Fourth, everyone would recognize that socialism was the hope of the future. Fifth, there would be socialist rule and the achievement of a full socialist world.

An alternative answer to the question of how socialism would be brought about was provided by believers in the ideas of Karl Marx. Marxists maintained that class conflict was the motor of human history and that capitalism would be replaced by socialism when the masses revolted against their oppressors. Marxism was brought to the United States, for the most part, by German immigrants. Until about 1895, American socialists who did not read German could not read Marx because there were no translations available; moreover, few explanations of Marx were printed in the American (or British) periodical press. But, while Karl Marx was largely unknown to him and to other socialists like him, Edward Bellamy, expressing a commonplace opinion, viewed the general idea of achieving social change through violent struggle as patently destructive and self-defeating. In the 24th chapter of *Looking Backward*, in fact, Bellamy had even argued that strikes were conspiracies of labor organizations and businesses to defeat efforts at reform.

"Nationalism" was supplanted in the 1890s by Populism and by forms of step-by-step electoral socialism. Populism, that is, the set of reform ideas and policies embraced by the People's Party, developed in the western states. It argued that the country was being taken over by east coast and European "moneychangers." It pressed for reforms in monetary policy, sought a graduated income tax, sought government ownership of railroads, the postal system, and the telegraph system, counseled direct legislation by voters through referendums, and argued in its 1896 "People's Party Platform" that during depressions "idle labor should be employed on public works as far as practicable." Populism did not last for more than a few years. Many of its supporters became participants in the "grassroots" socialist movement, oriented to the interests of farmers, that developed in midwest and southwest states in the 1890s. Wisconsin, Minnesota, North Dakota, Kansas, Colorado, and Oklahoma continued to be hotbeds of socialist sentiment well into the twentieth century; after it elected its first socialist mayor in 1908 and its first socialist US Congressman in 1910, Milwaukee came to be known as the most socialist city in the country.

Christian socialism, which claimed that Jesus was the first true socialist and that his social gospel should be followed, began to take root in the United States in the 1890s. American varieties of British "Fabian" socialism and the socialism contained in the Arts and Crafts movement led by William Morris also developed. Judging by remarks in socialist publications of the period and in letters and diaries, however, many self-described socialists did not think of themselves as belonging to this or that strain of the movement but, rather, as moral, decent people who wanted to bring about a better world through reforms. Their socialism, in short, meant making improvements. Making improvements, they thought, did not depend on having elaborate theories.

Marxists, who called themselves "scientific socialists" and prided themselves on their rigorous analytical abilities, argued that many non-Marxists were not socialists at all but confused members of the bourgeoisie, the oppressing class. For good measure, Marxists sometimes added that many non-Marxists, because they did not live in industrial cities, were living the "idiocy of rural life" that Marx had described in Germany. Remarks about rural "idiocy," like comments addressed to the peaceable about the need for class conflict and like quotations from Marx about religion being the "opiate" of the masses, did not produce many alliances between Marxists and other socialists.

Two socialist political parties emerged in the United States. The Socialist Labor Party, led by Daniel DeLeon, was rigorously Marxist, tiny, and ineffectual. Like the Democratic and Republican parties, the Socialist Party of America, founded in 1901, was a "big tent" party that attempted to serve as home to Marxists, non-Marxists, and virtually anybody else. It welcomed millionaires and coal miners, dentists and lawyers and day laborers, Fifth Avenue sophisticates and farmers, and people who just thought that socialism might be a good idea. The consequence of the "big tent" was that there was always intraparty debate about *how* socialism would be achieved, the role of violence, the nature of the working class, and so forth; and there was, as well, always tension between and among the leaders. Debates about the role of class conflict in bringing about social change seemed to arise every few years. They always ended, however, with the Party repudiating violence and calling for careful, committed, long-term work to achieve lasting results. Eugene Debs, the Party candidate for President of the United States in national elections in 1904, 1908, 1912, and 1920, conveyed the standard Party position when he remarked, in an article in the *International Socialist Review* in 1913, that the liberation of the working class would only occur as a result of "collective will" and that this will for change could only be achieved through "education, enlightenment, and self-imposed discipline." Debs added that he believed that the "collective reason of the workers repels the idea of individual violence where they are free to assert themselves by lawful and peaceful means."

However challenging its internal problems, the Socialist Party of America had many successes in the years between its beginning in 1901 and the US entry into World War I in 1917. It elected socialists to public office in some cities and states. It developed a substantial periodical press that got its message out to a large audience. It recruited some important writers, artists, and intellectuals to its cause. It became a fearless critic of corrupt government officials and of official stupidity. It introduced ideas, many of which had taken root in European countries, that were later adopted as national policy: for example, the creation of public works jobs for the unemployed, a shorter workday and workweek, and pensions for the elderly. It made, in short, an impressive beginning in what would later be called its "golden age."

The literature

It was generally recognized among all sectors of American society that the major influence on the lives of individuals was how they earned their living. The fundamental facts from which the union and socialist movements arose were the widespread recognition that great numbers of working people earned poverty-level wages, that "feudal" conditions prevailed in some industries, that many farmers suffered as much as industrial laborers, and that a very few people possessed most of the money and power. In turn-of-the-twentieth-century America, how work was done, how it was rewarded, what the overburdened lives of so many workers suggested about the reality of American social ideals, and many other related issues were summarized in the phrase "the labor question."

The labor question was the central issue in a significant number of classic literary works such as Edward Bellamy's *Looking Backward*, other utopian novels including William Dean Howells's *A Traveler from Altruria* (1894) and Charlotte Perkins Gilman's *Herland* (1915), the early work of Hamlin Garland, Upton Sinclair's *The Jungle* (1906), a number of novels by Jack London as well as his great short story "South of the Slot," and the most distinguished of Carl Sandburg's early poetry. The importance of work to individual well-being was a major consideration in Charlotte Perkins Gilman's "The Yellow Wall Paper."

I have already indicated that Bellamy's *Looking Backward* started the socialist movement known as Nationalism. The economic basis of Nationalism was the organization of all workers into an "industrial army," a concept that flowed logically, according to Bellamy, from the premise that the monopolies that controlled the business of the country should be taken over and "intrusted to a single syndicate representing the people, to be conducted in the common interest for the common profit." The new arrangement, which, astonishingly, produced no violent resistance from monopolists and their allies in Bellamy's novel, was called "The Great Trust," which as the nation's sole employer "simply applied the principle of universal military service, as it was understood in our own day, to the labor question."

Everyone in Bellamy's utopia underwent education until age 21. They then served in the industrial army for 24 years, the first three as common laborers. After those three years, they chose the work they wished to do for the rest of their service; if the job first chosen proved unsuitable, they could move into another job. Easy work demanded the longest hours; arduous work had very short hours. No wages were paid, and there were never complaints of injustice because the system required equal service from all. What would induce an individual to work hard and well? Bellamy said that "The army of industry is an army not alone by virtue of its perfect organization, but by reason also of the ardor of self-devotion which animates its members." These basic ideas and many related ones were elaborated on throughout *Looking Backward*, in the densely packed pages of the sequel that he later published, *Equality* (1897), in essays, in the magazine *The Nationalist*, and in meetings sponsored by the Nationalist clubs that were established across the country. For a few years, Bellamy and his disciples played a major role in the developing socialist movements.

Many disciples were educated, well-to-do women whose interests as women were specifically addressed in Chapter 25 of *Looking Backward*, where it was said that women were treated as the full equals of men in the new society. They were educated until age 21 and then served in the industrial army, though their needs and inclinations as women were to be appropriately respected. Women did not do degrading housework because of technological innovations and did not cook because all dining was in community dining halls. Most importantly, what Bellamy called the "root" of nineteenth-century women's "disability," their dependence on men, was replaced by independence and full personhood. Some of the complexities of women's traditional dependence were discussed in Chapter 23 of *Equality*, titled "What the Revolution Did for Women," where Bellamy described the "triple yoke" of bondage under which nineteenth-century women suffered: subjection to the personal and class rule of the rich, to the particular man on whom she depended, and to the traditional standards of how women should think, speak, and behave.

Underlying full personhood was the understanding that, for women as well as men, "labor, of a sort adapted to their powers, is well for body and mind, during the period of maximum physical vigor. We believe that the magnificent health which distinguishes our women … is owing largely to the fact that all alike are furnished with healthful and inspiriting occupation." Meaningful work, then, was the lynchpin for Nationalism.

Charlotte Perkins Gilman worked in the California branch of the Nationalist movement, giving nine lectures in early 1892 on "Why We Want Nationalism." Her great short story, "The Yellow Wall Paper," also published in 1892, owes a good deal to Bellamy's idea of the healthful effects of labor on women's lives as well as his idea of how women are crippled by their dependence on men. The well-to-do narrator of the story remarks that she believed that "congenial work, with excitement and change, would do me good" but is denied that possibility by her husband, who tries at every turn to insure her dependence on him. The result, echoing Bellamy again, is her sickliness.

Brilliantly narrated, "The Yellow Wall Paper" shows Gilman's masterful command of how the human mind works under extreme strains. In that regard, it is an even more sustained and acute accomplishment than either Ambrose Bierce's "Chickamauga" or Stephen Crane's *The Red Badge of Courage*, both of which were written within a few years of it. Gilman's accomplishment was recognized early in an article by Joseph Collins published in the *North American Review*. Collins wrote that Gilman had achieved an excellent presentation of the hallucinations brought on by exhaustion; he recognized that the character's problems also stemmed from her husband, a "literal, specific, standardized" man whose virtues she has "never admitted, even to herself … at times weigh heavily upon her."[2]

Signs of the continuing influence of Nationalism on Gilman occur regularly in her later writings, including her extensive discussions of the consequences of dependency and the promises of independence in her most widely known book, *Women and Economics* (1897). The Nationalist idea of the industrial army was adapted by Gilman in an article published in the *American Journal of Sociology*. Her suggestion was that those southern blacks "who are degenerating into an increasing percentage of social burdens or actual criminals" ought to be conscripted into a state-sponsored work army, given proper training and education, and afterwards do useful work as assigned by the state until they "graduated" and returned to live among their more socially evolved brethren.[3]

The need of well-to-do people for meaningful, healthful work was an occasional subject of discussion in the periodical press of the time, but deep interest in the work lives of ordinary people produced a great number of articles and books. Many were socialist in outlook and all of them were reformist. Pioneering books included Walter Wyckoff's *The Workers* (1898) and *A Day with a Tramp* (1901). Over several years, the *Independent* magazine published brief "life stories" of ordinary people. There was probably more writing about working women than about working men. In such books as Lillian Pettingill's *Toilers of the Home: The Record of a College Woman's Experiences as a Domestic Servant* (1903), educated middle-class women disguised themselves as ordinary workers, got hired, experienced the drudgery of manual labor, and then wrote about it. Dorothy Richardson's *The Long Day: The Story of a New York Working Girl* (1905) reported on the author's fall into millinery work from the lower reaches of the middle class. Among the accounts of women's work that used social science methods were Louise M. Bosworth's *The Living Wage of Women Workers* (1911), Elizabeth Beardsley Butler's *Saleswomen in Mercantile Stores* (1912), Mary Van Kleeck's *Artificial Flower Makers* (1913), and Katherine Anthony's *Mothers Who Must Earn* (1914).

---

[2]   Joseph Collins, "Lunatics of Literature," *North American Review*, 218 (September 1923), pp. 376–87.
[3]   Charlotte Perkins Gilman, "A Suggestion on the Negro Problem," *American Journal of Sociology*, 14 (July 1908), pp. 78–85.

Some of the literary works that I have commented on previously, such as Edwin Markham's "The Man With a Hoe," Hamlin Garland's *Main-Travelled Roads*, and Willa Cather's *O, Pioneers!* involved the work lives of farmers, and Gertrude Stein's *Three Lives*, read in its contemporary context, can be understood as, first of all, an effort to penetrate the psychologies of domestic workers. The perspectives of these writers varied. Garland was a Populist when he was writing his early stories, Markham was a socialist, while Stein and Cather were quite conservative and at times apolitical.

The most famous of the socialist writers was Upton Sinclair and the most famous of his works was *The Jungle*, a novel that was sometimes said to be the "*Uncle Tom's Cabin* of wage slavery." The novel was serialized in the weekly socialist newspaper *The Appeal to Reason*, which distributed most of its copies to rural subscribers, before it was issued as a book in 1906. The serialized version, the original text, was significantly toned down by Sinclair at the request of his publisher and was only recently reissued.

The Jungle tells the story of Jurgis Rudkus, a young Lithuanian who, with his extended family, migrates to the US, settles in Chicago, and has what Sinclair believes is the typical immigrant experience. That is, he is mistreated by uncaring employers and cheated by people who prey on his lack of experience. He and his family suffer poverty and hunger. His family dissolves as a result of one calamity after another and he becomes a drunkard. Along the way, Jurgis has a series of jobs and periods of unemployment. His first job is in one of Chicago's meatpacking factories. He then works in a fertilizer factory, in a farm equipment factory, in a steel mill, as a migrant farm laborer/hobo, as a construction laborer, as a criminal who serves time in jail, as a small-time politician, as a scab, as a foreman, and as a porter. His job in the farm equipment factory was a good one but it lasted for only eight days before the factory closed down. His job as a porter is actually as a *socialist* porter, for he is given it by socialist leaders following his conversion to socialism. The conversion occurs when he hears a speech by a charismatic socialist orator who looks and sounds like the real-life Eugene Debs.

Jurgis's story is punctuated by long and detailed expository passages in which Sinclair lays out the horrors of capitalist America, arguing that all work is exploitation, that profit is organized theft, and that no possibility for upward mobility exists for honest toilers. The passages have a didactic, instructional tone, teaching readers the facts about such things as how real estate people scam their clients; how business creates a surplus labor pool of unskilled immigrants; how workers are subjected to long hours, safety hazards, and pitifully poor pay; how women are sexually exploited in workplaces and elsewhere; how there is chronic unemployment and black-listing; how there is corruption at all levels of government; how saloons exercise their evil power over workingmen; and how the churches are irrelevant.

The parts of *The Jungle* focused on the Chicago meatpacking industry, about one-quarter of the book, contained graphic descriptions of factory killing floors, unhygienic production methods, and the hazardous, inhumane conditions under which men labored. A passage in Chapter 12 about the beef selected for canning was typical:

> It seemed that they must have agencies all over the country, to hunt out old and crippled and diseased cattle to be canned. There were cattle which had been fed on "whiskey malt," the refuse of the breweries, and had become what the men called "steerly" – which means covered with boils. It was a nasty job killing these, for when you plunged your knife into them they would burst and splash foul-smelling stuff into your face; and when a man's sleeves were smeared with blood, and his hands steeped in it, how was he ever to wipe his face, or to clear his eyes so that he could see?

The corrupt production practices of the industry had previously been exposed during the lengthy scandal following the documented poisoning of many soldiers and the deaths of some by contaminated tinned beef during the Spanish-American War; and as *The Jungle* was being written, the British medical journal *The Lancet* began publishing a series of articles on the industry as a public health danger. There was, then, a ready audience for the meatpacking parts of *The Jungle*, and that audience (and many later readers, too) was so riveted on disgusting food processing that it sometimes neglected the other parts of the book, forgetting Sinclair's main points about how capitalism destroyed the lives of its workers. Regarding this limited reading of his book, Sinclair remarked that he had aimed for his reader's hearts but had "hit their stomachs."

The pure food movement, which was at the time arguing for vegetarianism and government regulation of processed foods, found an ally in Sinclair, and *The Jungle* was said to have had an important impact on the development of the Pure Food and Drug Act of 1906. So, too, Temperance advocates of the time could have discovered a kindred spirit in Sinclair, for

The Jungle contained important antialcohol and antisaloon elements, as I indicated earlier in this chapter.

That the novel contained so many disparate ideological threads did not displease some socialists. For, from their perspectives, the socialist movement, especially in its formative stages, needed to be a big tent which sheltered people with diverse interests and motivations, a place of coalitions between moderates who believed in winning elections, revolutionists, Temperance advocates, craft unionists, progressive vegetarians, women's suffrage advocates, and so forth.

From another perspective, on the other hand, that of the Industrial Workers of the World (IWW), such diversity created too much talk and too little action, gave too much power to educated, articulate people, and maintained, against all reason, that socialist lawyers, professors, and social workers had the same class interests as miners, factory hands, and migrant workers. According to this way of thinking, the movement needed to cast away its educated professionals, its rational Bellamyites, anyone who thought electing politicians was the way to bring fundamental change to the country, anyone who didn't understand that a bucket of beer and a good steak were basic elements of red-blooded working-class culture, and anyone who believed that workers needed to hear speeches by socialist orators and to read books by socialist writers in order to conclude that they were exploited and needed to take action. Moderate socialists answered, as could be expected, that these militant ideas did not add up to socialism at all but to wild unionism or anarchism.

Among writers, Sinclair was one of the big tent moderate socialists, as was Charlotte Perkins Gilman. Jack London advocated different socialisms at different times but in a story like "South of the Slot," he clearly opted for the IWW brand. Carl Sandburg, who began his socialist career as a moderate, later switched his allegiance and became a major propagandist for the IWW press under his own name and under a number of pseudonyms while simultaneously writing his most famous poetry, including "Chicago."

In Bellamy, Sinclair, and a great number of other moderate socialist writers, workers were nearly always presented as victims of capitalist exploitation. They were beaten down by the "system." They were bedraggled, bent, and worn out. Any hope the poor victims had was likely as not to come in the form of a great and wise leader, or a political party or movement, who carried them over to a brave new world in the making. There were no bedraggled victims in IWW-inspired writing like "South of the

Slot" and Sandburg's early poems. Instead, there were tough and strong workers who knew how to take care of themselves and did not need anyone from a higher class to show them the way.

"South of the Slot" was first published in the family-oriented weekly magazine *The Saturday Evening Post* in May 1909. Its main character is Freddie Drummond, "a college man, in dress and carriage as like as a pea to the type that of late years is being so generously turned out of our institutions of higher learning." Freddie is now a University of California sociology professor who specializes in doing time-and-motion studies of industrial workers and writing books theorizing about how to prevent their on-the-job malingering and get the most production out of them. As London describes them, his books, with titles like *The Fallacy of the Inefficient*, sound as if they could have been written by another Freddie, Frederick Winslow Taylor, the so-called "father" of early twentieth-century scientific management and the master of time-and-motion investigations. No doubt, London was treating his readers to an ironic caricature of the very famous Taylor.

Like other writers about work, Freddie Drummond disguises himself as an ordinary worker in order to do his research. Before long, in a comic twist, he finds that he enjoys the life of the working class and, using the pseudonym of "Big Bill Totts" (a clear allusion to Big Bill Haywood, the IWW leader), becomes known among his fellow workers as a man "who could drink and smoke, and slang and fight, and be an all-around favorite." Big Bill lives in the present, unable and uninterested in seeing "beyond the next meal and the prize-fight the next night at the Gaiety Athletic Club," working as a longshoreman, hanging out in saloons, eating lots of sausages and oysters, laughing loudly and heartily, hating scabs, fighting, and wooing Mary Condon, a hot, tough, and uninhibited union president. Big Bill sometimes disappears and goes to his university as Freddie to teach his sociology classes, write his books, and prepare to marry the college-educated, very proper, and inhibited Catherine Van Vorst, the daughter of the wealthy head of the Philosophy Department. The resolution of the strange doubleness of Freddie-Big Bill comes at the end when Freddie becomes Big Bill, jumps into the middle of a wild fight between strikers and the policemen protecting a group of scabs, is hailed as the mob's "champion," and walks off with Mary Condon into the "labor ghetto," leaving an amazed Catherine Van Vorst behind.

"South of the Slot" is a comic celebration of the vitality of working-class culture and two-fisted unionist direct action and a condemnation of antiunion upper-class collegiate culture and its life-negating fixations on efficiency, sobriety, respectability, and order. Similar celebrations of strong and tough workers appear in Carl Sandburg's first book, *Chicago and Other Poems* (1916). The most famous poem in that book, "Chicago," has always been read as a kind of booster poem for the city. But the poem's chief element was the personification of Chicago as a tough worker who loomed "half naked" above the skyline "with lifted head singing so proud to be / alive and coarse and strong and cunning." He was a "a tall bold slugger," primal, elemental. He stood with "dust all over his mouth, laughing with white teeth" and "Laughing even as an ignorant fighter laughs who has never lost a battle." In "Dynamiter," set in a saloon where the speaker and his friend the dynamiter eat steak and onions, Sandburg extols the joyful, red-blooded humanity of a union man who is known for blowing things up. In "Ice Handler," the setting is also a saloon and the union man celebrated has a "hard pair of fists," spends a dollar every Saturday night on a big woman who works as a dishwasher, and tells stories about breaking the noses of two scabs and sabotaging scab wagons. In "Jack," the old man extolled in a sort of obituary is said to have had hands "tougher than shoe leather," raised eight children, lost the "tough woman" who had been his wife, hears infrequently from his children, but nonetheless "There was joy on his face when he died as there was joy on his face when he lived – he was a swarthy, swaggering son-of-a-gun."

A Brief Note about the Place of Black Americans in Social Change Movements

For the most part, black Americans found no place in the Temperance movement, the craft union movement, or in the various socialist movements.

Those northern Temperance women who might have found it in their hearts and interests to include black women in their crusades against drink deferred to southern white women and refused entrance to their black sisters. Black women formed their own Temperance organizations.

The American Federation of Labor organized craft workers. The skilled crafts, some of which were more or less monopolized by particular ethnic groups, and in many of which apprenticeships and jobs were passed down within families from generation to generation, were not open to black men.

The Socialist Party of America was consistently and purely *economic* in its analysis and orientation. It reasoned that the oppressions of race (and gender, too) would end after the revolution and thus made no special efforts to recruit blacks as a group, though there *were* some black members and sympathizers. Some SPA documents, however, suggest racist motivations and outlooks. There was the racist diatribe in *The Jungle* that I quoted in Chapter 2. There were occasional comments in the SPA press about how members should not also be Ku Klux Klan members, an indication that some people thought otherwise. There were also occasional essays and speeches, such as the one given by the great socialist organizer Kate Richards O'Hare in 1912. In it, O'Hare offered a one-word solution to the "race question." That word was "segregation," which meant giving blacks "one section of the country" as their own and letting them develop their own civilization.[4]

The IWW often stated that it was color-blind and it successfully organized Chinese, Mexican, and black workers. On occasion, though, a leader like Big Bill Haywood was not averse to using racist rhetoric to rouse a white audience, as when, in a very famous 1912 speech, he spoke of how black soldiers had put white union men behind a barbed wire enclosure during a strike and then went to the homes of the strikers where they were seen "insulting, outraging, ravishing their wives, mothers, sisters, and sweethearts."[5]

[4] Kate Richards O'Hare, "'Nigger' Equality," *National Ripsaw*, 4 (March 25, 1912), p. 40.
[5] William D. Haywood, "Socialism the Hope of the Working Class," *International Socialist Review*, 12 (1912), p. 467.

7

Culminations
From the US Entry into World War I to 1929

The Context

Consequences of the Great War

World War I, or, as it was known to contemporaries, the "Great War," which began in August 1914 and ended in November 1918, killed about 16 million soldiers and several million civilians. Millions more were wounded. A vast land area in Europe was devastated. And as the war was winding down in the summer and early fall of 1918, 30 million more people died worldwide, by conservative estimates, in an influenza pandemic.

For much of the war, the United States was officially neutral. But in April 1917, the US declared war on Germany and its allies. By war's end, according to the US Department of Veterans Affairs, about 125,000 Americans had been killed, 53,000 in battle and the rest primarily as a result of accident and influenza. Another 204,000 were wounded. About 700 American civilians also died in the conflict. United States casualties were far lower than European casualties. But, because of wartime domestic events and policies, the effects of the war were long-lasting and deep.

The American declaration of war led to patriotic displays and also to expressions of antiwar sentiment. Some immigrant groups resisted military service. Jews, for example, were not enthusiastic about fighting in a war in which the US was allied with Russia, from which so many had fled, nor were Irish-Americans happy about fighting on the same side as the British, who were at the time continuing their domination of Ireland through the brutal repression of the latest Irish rebellion. Pacifists and some Christian groups, led by Mennonites and Quakers, spoke out forcefully against participating in the European slaughter. Some radicals argued vehemently against the shedding of American working-class blood in a war between capitalists over markets and access to resources. The Socialist Party of America took, arguably, the most uncompromising position of any of the antiwar groups. Shortly after war was declared, it issued its own "Declaration," pledging its members to "continuous, active, and public opposition to the war through demonstrations, mass petitions, and all other means within our power" and vowed "vigorous resistance to all reactionary measures, such as censorship of press and mails, restriction of the right of free speech, assemblage, and organization, or compulsory arbitration and limitation of the right to strike."

Labor did in fact exercise its "right" to strike. Between April and October 1917, just as war production was being stepped up, "strike fever" increased across the country. Sectors deeply involved in the war effort, such as copper mining, metal trades, and shipbuilding, were among the most affected, and, with a total of nearly six million workdays lost to strikes in that seven-month period, a new record was set for strike participation by workers. The radical Industrial Workers of the World was involved in one-sixth of these strikes, which caused it to increase its rhetoric about impending revolution. This made it seem to some observers that the organization, as well as other striking unions, was conspiring to bring down the government.

The Wilson Administration, Congress, and the mainstream press under-stood that the war effort depended on patriotism, on complete "100 percent Americanism," as the phrase of the day expressed it. Therefore, in a move that would reverberate for decades, government officials and their support-ers soon began to define any spoken or written dissent from the war effort as *prima facie* evidence of the dissenter's treasonous anti-Americanism. Furthermore, it was understood that the war effort also depended on the stable, predictable production of goods, so any strike or on-the-job action that stopped or slowed production was defined by government officials and their supporters as evidence of subversion.

The Federal government passed important war legislation. In April 1917, the Liberty Loan Act was passed. One of the effects of this piece of legislation was the beginning of a government drive to get citizens to purchase bonds to fund the war. This drive caused the production of a tremendous amount of material by the Federal Bureau of Propaganda. Prowar articles written by Bureau operatives were planted in newspapers; beautifully illustrated war posters filled public spaces, promoting the purchase of bonds, encouraging support of the troops, warning against subversion, and excoriating the blood-thirsty German army. In May, because voluntary enlistments in the armed services were insufficient, the government passed the Selective Service Act. This bill criminalized any young men who failed to register for the draft. In June, an act even more significant than the Liberty Loan Act or Selective Service Act was passed. The Espionage Act imposed fines of up to $10,000 and jail sentences of up to 20 years on persons convicted of aiding the enemy or obstructing recruiting for the armed services. The Act also gave the Postmaster General of the United States the authority to bar from the mails any treasonous or seditious materials.

Dissent from the war, whether uttered in speech or put into writing, was thus outlawed. Because the Department of Justice ceded to local police authorities the power to arrest antiwar speakers, and because the US Postmaster General ceded to local postal authorities his power to prevent magazines and newspapers from being sent to subscribers through the mails, getting the antiwar message out became virtually impossible.

The Federal government was unrelenting in its pursuit of dissenters. Augmenting the powers it had given itself through the Espionage Act, it passed the Sedition Act in May 1918. This made it a criminal offense to "utter, print, write, or publish any disloyal, profane, scurrilous, or abusive language about the government, the Constitution, or the uniform of the army or navy."

The government also worked undercover to stifle dissent. By the summer of 1917, the Bureau of Investigation of the Department of Justice, as well as the Military Intelligence Division of the US Army, had begun to undertake systematic surveillance of radicals and other dissenters. Surveillance activities included the infiltration of antiwar organizations, the surreptitious searching of offices to pilfer incriminating evidence, and the opening of mail written to or by targeted individuals. None of these surveillance efforts were known to targets at the time, though some must have suspected because discoveries made through surveillance were used in Espionage Act prosecutions.

The Federal government effort to prevent the expression of antiwar sentiments was uniformly successful. Prosecutions under the Espionage and Sedition Acts yielded long jail terms for both ordinary perpetrators and famous people such as the Socialist Party leader Kate Richards O'Hare and the perennial Socialist Party presidential candidate Eugene V. Debs. Furthermore, at the grassroots level in many communities, vigilantes attacked dissenters and others deemed not to be "100 percent American." Some organized groups such as the Ku Klux Klan used the government prowar effort as an opportunity to mount rhetorical as well as direct action campaigns against Jews, Catholics, blacks, and others who did not meet the 100 percent standard.

A large and influential radical press had developed in the first two decades of the twentieth century. Among the more important magazines were the *International Socialist Review,* published in Chicago; Emma Goldman's *Mother Earth,* published in Greenwich Village in Manhattan; and *The Masses,* edited by John Reed, Floyd Dell, and Max Eastman, also published in Greenwich Village. *Mother Earth* and *The Masses* were important not just to the radical union and political movements; they were also magazines which sponsored radical writing and radical lifestyles. At the beginning of each issue of *The Masses,* a brief manifesto was printed saying that the magazine was "directed against rigidity and dogma wherever it was found" and that it was a magazine "whose final policy is to do as it pleases and conciliate no one, not even its readers." Like *Mother Earth,* *The Masses* always argued for mass revolt, passion, confrontation, and radical energy, and it became a force especially among young artists and writers. It published important work including for example, Sherwood Anderson's "Hands" in its March 1916 issue. John Reed, who had begun his career hoping to be a poet but soon turned to journalism, becoming very adept at strike reporting, seemed to many to symbolize the period's youthful spirit of revolt.

Using a variety of legal devices, the government moved to close down the dissenting radical press. By the fall of 1918, it was completely successful.

The radical Industrial Workers of the World came in for special treatment by "private citizens" as well as local, state, and Federal governments. Especially in the upper Far West and the Southwest, IWW members were prime targets. In Bisbee, Arizona, several hundred IWW miners were rounded up by local people, packed onto freight cars, and carried into the desert, where they were unloaded and told to fend for themselves. Eventually, they had to be rescued from the desert heat by a contingent of US Army troops. In Butte, Montana, as told in one eyewitness account by a government surveillance agent, IWW organizer Frank Little was forcibly taken from his rooming house in the middle of the night by locals, then castrated and hung from a railroad trestle. Bisbee and Butte were but two instances among many such outrages.

The IWW lost its "class war" on the ground. It also lost it in the courts. In September 1917, during the record-breaking "strike fever" which followed the American entrance into the war, Federal agents conducted coordinated raids against the IWW, destroying offices in many localities and arresting large numbers of actual and suspected Wobblies. One hundred prominent IWW members – essentially, its entire leadership – were charged with disloyalty, encouraging draft resistance, and other crimes. They were tried *en masse* in Chicago. The evidence against them was IWW writing and speeches. Of the 100 defendants found guilty, 15 got 20-year jail terms, 35 got 10-year terms, 33 got five-year terms, and the other 17 received nominal terms. In a parallel case tried under state statutes in California, 53 Wobblies were charged. All were jailed together in one 21 x 21 foot cell in Sacramento while awaiting trial. Five died before the beginning of the trial. The others were found guilty and given long jail terms.

The widespread, virtually complete suppression of radicals and other dissenters as a result of the Great War, and the elevation of "100 percent Americanism" to the status of a core national policy, was furthered by the effects of the fall 1917 Bolshevik Revolution in Russia. Reports of the initial successes of the Revolution produced fear and loathing in the American government and business enterprises. That fear and loathing was compounded in April 1918 when, needing to turn its attention to the civil war which had broken out in Russia between the "red" Bolsheviks and the counterrevolutionary "whites," the Bolsheviks signed a "separate peace" with Germany and thus withdrew its armies from the Great War (pre-Bolshevik, Czarist Russia had been a crucial ally of France, Great Britain, and the US). The fear and loathing was probably doubled, at least, when it became clear that the Bolsheviks thought of their revolution as an international, not a Russian, phenomenon. By the time of the November 1918 Armistice ending the Great War, the Bolsheviks had already made significant efforts to spread the revolution across Europe. Shortly after the Armistice, the Bolshevik leader, Vladimir Ilich Lenin, wrote a "Letter to American Workingmen," smuggled into the United States by the journalist-poet Carl Sandburg and later published, which said that it was now time for American workers to follow the Bolshevik example.

The Bolshevik Revolution had enduring effects on American foreign and domestic policy. The immediate domestic effect in the last months of the Great War and in its immediate aftermath was to make it even easier to attack and suppress American dissenters. Some radicals were deeply sympathetic to Bolshevism, announcing their support publicly. John Reed happened to be in Russia at the time of the Revolution, and wrote a sympathetic account of it titled *Ten Days That Shook The World* (1919). But all radicals, regardless of their actual beliefs, their opponents claimed, were guilty of Bolshevism by association. Was the radical against the war effort, did the radical wish to bring about equality and social justice, did the radical wish to bring about "industrial democracy" and an end to business "feudalism," did the radical believe in "class warfare," did the radical believe in "free love" as opposed to the "sanctity" of marriage? The answers were, in many cases, of course "Yes!" Did Bolsheviks believe these things? Again, the answer was "Yes!" So, therefore, obviously, opponents claimed, radicals and other dissenters were Bolsheviks. Did anyone notice the logical flaw in the argument? Surely. But questioning the logic was not done often because questioning was itself a form of predissent, so to speak, which could get the questioner tagged as a Bolshevik.

Throughout 1919, there were virtually daily press reports of the impending collapse of Bolshevism in Russia and some contradictory reports of the frightening gains made by Bolsheviks. Largely unreported in the US was the entrance of some 7,000 American soldiers into Russia, where they, along with British and French troops, were allied with the "white" counterrevolutionaries.

But Bolshevism alone did not dominate the news, and in fact 1919 was, arguably, the worst year in American history up to that point in terms of ugly, destructive, and unsettling events. Through the year, what had become routine and standard repressions of radicals, dissenters, and unions continued apace, with Attorney General A. Mitchell Palmer orchestrating raids and arrests. An attempt to pay Palmer back was made in June: his family home was targeted by anarchist bombers, but the bomb exploded as it was being placed and only killed the anarchist, Carlo Valdiroci. Meanwhile, new records were set for the number of strikes and the number of workdays lost because of strikes: four million workers, one-fifth of the total workforce, were on strike at some point in the year. The most significant of the strikes were a strike by policemen in Boston, a general strike in Seattle, and the so-called Great Steel Strike involving 365,000 steel workers. Each of these strikes led to martial law declarations and big losses for unions. In addition to the strikes, between May and October, 1919 there were some two dozen race riots in the country, with considerable loss of life and property. Many of the riots were in northern cities, a fact that gave the lie to the notion that American racism was a southern phenomenon.

In the autumn, following the strikes and the bombings and the race riots, an event occurred which may have struck the majority of Americans as more tragic and painful than the goings-on with Bolsheviks and bombers, unions and blacks. Several members of the Chicago White Sox, having been reached by gamblers ("Jewish gamblers," according to some accounts), threw the World Series in what became known as the "Black Sox Scandal." In December, on the other hand, many Americans must have breathed considerably easier when they learned that some 240 alien anarchists, including Emma Goldman and Alexander Berkman, had been deported to Europe aboard the SS Buford, also known as the "Red Ark," after Department of Justice proceedings.

While radicalism in the United States was clearly defeated, business leaders, politicians, and the press played up the continuing threat by constantly promoting "100 percent Americanism" and the need for vigilance as the 1920s began. Events such as the "Wall Street Bombing" of September 16, 1920, seemed to prove their point. On that occasion, which occurred in the midst of a presidential campaign, a huge bomb was set off on Wall Street near the stock exchange, severely damaging several buildings, killing 40 people, and injuring hundreds more. The bombers were never caught, though there was, it was claimed, clear evidence pointing at a group of Italian anarchists living in the country. A few months before the Wall Street Bombing, a robbery and murders had occurred in South Braintree, Massachusetts, for which two Italian immigrants, Nicola Sacco and Bartolomeo Vanzetti, were later arrested, convicted at a trial that seemed to many to have been presided over by a prejudiced judge and to have had weak evidence, and eventually executed in 1927. The Sacco and Vanzetti case became a international *cause célèbre* involving a number of American writers.

There would be continuing outbreaks of labor "unrest" and sporadic riots against blacks in the next several years. But Warren G. Harding, the first of three consecutive deeply conservative Republican presidents, probably caught the mood and desires of the majority of the country in his 1920 campaign speech, "A Return to Normalcy." Harding argued for tradition, calm, and a withdrawal from international involvements: "America's present need is not heroics, but healing; not nostrums, but normalcy; not revolution but restoration; not agitation, but adjustment; not surgery, but serenity; not the dramatic, but the dispassionate; not experiment, but equipoise; not submergence in internationality, but sustainment in triumphant nationality." In specific passages, he argued for an end to "false economics" which led to "chaos" and for "quality of citizenship" as opposed to the notion that human ills could be cured by government legislation. Harding won the Presidency with more than 60 percent of the vote, carrying 37 states (the Democrats won 11 southern states).

Apparent resolutions of old conflicts

Many of the long-standing domestic policy conflicts were seemingly settled between 1919 and 1929:

- As already indicated, radicalism in all of its forms was defeated.
- The manufacture, sale, and transportation of "intoxicating liquors" was finally banned in the United States as a result of the ratification of the 18th Amendment to the Constitution on January 16, 1919. The ban went into effect one year after that date.
- Women were finally given full voting rights as a result of the ratification of the 19th Amendment to the Constitution on August 26, 1920.
- Legislation restricting immigration began with the Immigration Act of 1917, which established an "Asiatic Barred Zone," a broad area including India, Afghanistan, Arabia, parts of East Asia and the Pacific. No laborers from this zone were permitted entry into the US. Restrictive legislation continued with the First Quota Act of 1921, which fixed the annual number of people of particular national groups allowed to immigrate. The quotas were lowered in 1924 and again in 1929. The 1929 legislation, called the National Origins Quota Act, set the annual ceiling for immigration from northern and western Europe at 127,000, set the annual ceiling for immigration from southern and eastern Europe at 21,000, and banned Asian immigration altogether. Immigration by people born in Western Hemisphere countries was not restricted under the quota system.
- The political popularity of 100 percent Americanism gave added impetus to the Ku Klux Klan which, especially in the first half of the 1920s, displayed a good deal of political power (a November 1923 *New York Times* article reported that the Klan now controlled politics in Oregon, Indiana. Arkansas, and Texas and was making big gains in other states). The Klan also seemed for a while poised to enter the business of university education in order to teach "pure Americanism" to students, as reported in the *New York Times* in September 1921; a July

1923 *Times* article discussed the Klan's effort, ultimately unsuccessful, to take over Valparaiso University in Indiana).[1]

- Anti-Jewish sentiment crested in the 1920s. Even Jews who had lived in the US for decades faced increased resistance from the KKK, from other organized groups, and from their fellow citizens who belonged to no groups at all.

Prosperity

In 1921 the United States struggled through what was called at the time an economic depression. In the following seven to eight years, the economy boomed. Newspapers, magazines, business leaders, economists, and politicians wrote and spoke with enthusiasm and great pride about the magical and amazing "New Prosperity."

Declarations about the dizzying wealth of the country were commonplace, especially after 1926. For example, in August of that year the *New York Times*, which throughout the period was virtually the only source of national economic news, published a long article by Stuart Chase which declared that the current prosperity was the greatest the world had ever seen. In the last fiscal year, Chase said, American factories, mines, and workshops had outpaced all prior production records and Americans now owned 40 percent of the world's wealth. A similar note was struck in a November 1927 *Times* article by Evans Clark, which reported that General Motors, the auto manufacturer, had just declared the largest single stock dividend in the history of the world and that government data indicated that the American economy produced twice as many goods and services as the combined economies of Great Britain, France, Germany, Italy, and Belgium. It was also reported that the US per capita income, according to the government, was now $766, compared to the per capita incomes of $417 in England, $192 in France, $168 in Germany, and $119 in Italy.[2]

---

[1] "Klan's Shadow Falls on Nation's Politics," *New York Times*, November 18, 1923, p. xx3; "Forrest Tells Aim of Ku Klux College," *New York Times*, September 12, 1921, p. 12; "A Klan University," *New York Times*, July 28, 1923, p. 6.

[2] Stuart Chase, "America's Wealth Reaches New Height," *New York Times*, August 22, 1926, p. xx1; Evans Clark, "America's Prosperity Reaches New Heights," *New York Times*, November 27, 1927, p. xx4.

To virtually all commentators, the "New Prosperity" was most clearly and easily seen in the sharp increase of consumer goods. It was common to celebrate the increasing ownership of automobiles and telephones as the great signposts of prosperity (Stuart Chase said that in 1926 there were 20 million automobiles in the country and 16 million telephones, both astounding numbers). William T. Ogburn, Professor of Sociology at the University of Chicago and President of the American Sociological Society, told *Times* readers in August 1929 that 50 percent of all the world's radios, 60 percent of its telephones, and 80 percent of its automobiles were in the United States. He predicted a future in which Americans would live in homes crammed with even greater numbers of technological gadgets and devices.[3] Professor Ogburn's optimistic statement came, of course, less than two months before the stock market crash began the Great Depression.

In later years, literary critics and others referred to the 1920s as the Jazz Age, the Roaring Twenties, and the Age of Prosperity. None of the commentators I have cited was so sanguine or enthusiastic, nor did any believe that poverty had been eliminated by the "New Prosperity." Professor Ogburn recognized that while the 1920s had produced a higher standard of living for American workers generally, there were big differences in the pay of skilled and unskilled workers. Stuart Chase remarked that "poverty is far from eliminated." Evans Clark wrote that prosperity was enjoyed by some sectors but not others. Drawing on government reports, he added that there continued to be a severe "depression" in American agriculture; the wages of government workers, clerical workers and laborers were "still below par"; and that coal miners and cotton mill workers had seen little improvement in their wages. While such comments may not have been noticed by boosters and superficial readers because they appeared as mere caveats to the big good news of prosperity, whole articles about poverty in the midst of plenty were published in major magazines.[4]

During his successful 1928 presidential election campaign, Republican Herbert Hoover said on many occasions that under his two Republican predecessors, Warren G. Harding and Calvin Coolidge, prosperity had

---

[3] William T. Ogburn, "Our Standard of Living Viewed as Going Higher," *New York Times*, August 25, 1929, p. xx11.

[4] For example, "Prosperity, for Whom," *Nation*, 120 (February 18, 1925), p. 174; "Too Much Prosperity," *New Republic*, 42 (March 18, 1925), pp. 88–9; "Whose Prosperity is This," *Independent*, 118 (March 12, 1927), p. 281; "Another Year of Selective Prosperity," *Literary Digest*, 93 (April 9, 1927), pp. 82–6.

prevailed and that poverty had decreased so much that "we are now within hope" of abolishing it.[5] Even before his inauguration, he began to take steps to lay the groundwork for fulfilling the hope of abolishing poverty by appointing a committee to study recent economic changes in the US. Emphasizing his serious purpose, Hoover named himself as chairman. The committee was bipartisan, progressive, and friendly to the cause of organized labor and working people generally. Members included William Green, President of the American Federation of Labor; John J. Raskob, Chairman of the Democratic National Committee; Owen D. Young, Chairman of the Board of the General Electric Corporation; Max Mason, Director of the Rockefeller Foundation's Division of Natural Sciences; Louis J. Taber, the head of the farmers' organization, the National Grange; and Daniel Willard, the head of the Baltimore and Ohio Railroad. These were all men of tremendous accomplishment and fame. At the time, though, Young and Willard were probably the most widely respected. Young was applauded for inaugurating and presiding over GE corporate policies that gave employees access to pensions, home mortgage loans, life insurance, unemployment insurance, and a profit-sharing plan. Willard was widely respected as a man who had made his corporation into a virtual management–labor cooperative enterprise and for providing his employees with great job security, respect, and improved working conditions.

Hoover's committee reported its findings in mid-1929 in a dense two-volume, 950-page treatise titled *Recent Economic Changes in the United States*. Written by experts who worked at such places as the National Bureau of Economic Research, the American Engineering Council, Harvard University, Cornell University, and the Federal Reserve Bank, it bristled with statistical tables and graphs that many readers would have had a great deal of difficulty understanding. But the book began with a clear introductory summary of some of the findings, and that summary was widely reprinted in newspapers. Its major points included the following:

- The committee members were struck by the "outpouring of energy" of the last seven years. The energy was manifested in the nation's 20,000 miles of airways, 25 million autos, and 17 million electrified homes. In addition, almost four million students now attended high school and another million were in college.

---

[5] See, for example, "Hoover Goes West: Stresses Prosperity to Maryland Crowd," *New York Times*, November 2, 1928, p. 1.

- The activity of the last seven years had been "spotty." Some industries had progressed while others had declined or had been in a state of "depression." Among the problematic industries were cotton manufacture, grain farming, and coal mining. Some wholesalers and retailers had been under "grave economic pressure." There had been significant "technological" unemployment, that is, significant displacement of workers by "improved machinery and methods."
- The densely populated New England and Middle Atlantic states had experienced "difficulties in adapting their older industries to new conditions." Other parts of the country had done well.
- Industries and managements had developed more efficient methods of production and distribution. Efficient electric power was now widely available to industry. Credit had become increasingly available to businesses.
- There had been a widespread rise in the standard of living. There were widely available facilities and services that increased the comfort and well-being of people: low-priced autos, radio entertainment, improved transportation and communication systems, and so forth. The wants of Americans, their desire for consumable goods and services, had expanded dramatically. People had an "almost insatiable appetite for goods and services." Beyond food, clothing, and shelter, an increasing number of families now had an appetite for "optional consumption." Increasing leisure had led to increasing interest in the fine arts, books and magazines, movies, science, foreign travel, education, sports, and tourism.

Even the introductory summary of *Recent Economic Changes* suggested that all boats had not risen on the tide of the "New Prosperity." Readers who worked their way through the actual two-volume study, however, would have discovered more cheerless commentaries about the recent experience of major parts of the American population. The summary mentioned that certain economic sectors had declined, but it did not indicate the degree to which the largest of them, farming, had suffered.

Some 20 percent of employed Americans were farmers, and farm families, because they tended to be relatively large, comprised about 30 percent of the country's population. As it had been for decades, farming in the 1920s was extremely troubled, beset by inefficiencies, intense competition, high debt burdens, and low profits. The author of the chapter on "Agriculture" in *Recent Economic Changes* summarized the situation succinctly: "farmers have suffered severely in the years since 1920 and are still finding recovery slow and rather unsatisfactory. The process of readjustment is too fundamental and far-reaching to be accomplished in any short period of time. Furthermore, we must not forget that the so-called depression in agriculture is … an international problem." Statements like that, however, would have shocked few during the 1920s. The country's agricultural press and regional newspapers had been pointing out for years that prosperity had not touched the vast majority of farmers. Even the big city national press had reported on the farm depression. In January 1927 the *New York Times*, for instance, ran a long story in which farm foreclosures and the collapse of rural banks was described. The story also included remarks that suggested that the reporter and his readers were keen to indulge old city–country tensions. Capable youngsters, it was reported, were being drawn away from farming. A study of rural communities in Indiana had recently found that, after generations of out-migration, as many as 27 percent of children in rural schools were "feeble-minded"; the IQ average of Indiana city students was 100, while the average for rural students was 77.[6] As could be expected, in the chapter on "Agriculture" in *Recent Economic Changes*, "strident assertions" about the declining quality of farm populations were dismissed as, at best, the sort of confused thinking that resulted from exposure to farmers only in certain backward areas of the country and not in places where farmers were moving forward. The author of the chapter also cited the work of a US Department of Agriculture expert about migrations out of farmlands and migrations into farmlands from cities (a phenomenon that was usually ignored by journalists). The conclusion of that expert was that the net loss of farm population between 1920 and 1927 was probably three million.

James J. Davis was Secretary of Labor in the Harding, Coolidge, and Hoover Administrations. In the later 1920s, he made many speeches in which he said that the American worker had never been better off. Speaking to a union audience in Florida on October 2, 1928, for instance, he used his standard language to summarize the progress that had recently been made, saying that the poor were getting richer and holding out the possibility that poverty could be "conquered."[7] Secretary Davis, incidentally, had

---

[6]   Evans Clark, "The Farm Issue Moves Toward a Climax: American Agriculture, Poverty-Stricken Amid Prodigious Commercial Activity, Has Now Reached Front of National Stage – The Extent and Cause of the Long Farm Depression Analyzed," *New York Times*, January 2, 1927, p. xx1.
[7]   "Sees 'Poor Getting Richer,'" *New York Times*, October 2, 1928, p.52.

extensive and deep personal knowledge of poverty and the possibilities available to working people. He had been born in Wales, had migrated with his family to the US, and his earlier working years had been spent in the Pittsburgh steel mills, as he told the public in *The Iron Puddler: My Life in the Rolling Mills and What Came of It* (1922), the autobiography he published shortly after he became Secretary of Labor.

But Secretary Davis usually emphasized that while things had improved, much still needed to be done. On Memorial Day, 1929, for example, speaking to a crowd of thousands in Gettysburg, Pennsylvania, he said that Americans needed to rededicate themselves to abolishing the "slavery" that still existed in the land. While there was ample opportunity for men of the working class to rise to higher positions, there were still "many" Americans who were "insufficiently paid for their toil," who still lived "enslaved" lives, and he asked his audience to join with him in a new emancipation movement.[8]

Several months before his Gettysburg speech, Davis wrote a widely publicized letter to the editor of a newspaper in Wales in which he recognized that a million Welsh miners were on the verge of starvation. In it, he deplored the idea, current among Europeans, he said, that because of prosperity America had become a utopia for workers. No foreign impression of American had ever been more false, he wrote, and he speculated that the false impression was based on the fact that Europeans only met traveling Americans who were rich or well-to-do. In reality, he wrote, the country was no utopia, for 86 percent of Americans were poor and shared in the worldwide "brotherhood of poverty."[9] Eighty-six percent of Americans were poor? Eighty-six percent of Americans were poor after several years of the "New Prosperity"? For many readers, that must have seemed to have been a colossal error, either by Davis himself or by the *Times*. But no correction was forthcoming.

The Literature

No 1920s writer that I have ever read joined in the celebrations of the postwar era's "return to normalcy," or the suppression of political dissent, or prosperity, or the 1920s culture of extreme consumption, or Prohibition,

---

[8] "Secretary Davis Asks Changes in Industry," *New York Times*, May 31, 1929, p. 4.

[9] "86 P.C. Here Poor, Davis Tells Europe," *New York Times*, January 20, 1929, p. 3.

or the efforts to bring about a "purer" nation. Instead, the classic literature of the period, and much of the minor literature, depicts a deeply troubled, inauthentic, corrupted culture. Very often, the classics written during the period – for example, F. Scott Fitzgerald's *The Great Gatsby*, Willa Cather's *The Professor's House*, Ernest Hemingway's short stories and *The Sun Also Rises* – also suggest that individuals who have experienced the corrupted America need to leave it behind if they are going to have any chance to discover their authentic selves or to discover the place where authenticity exists. These attitudes about life in the US were not unusual. They were occasionally voiced in the popular press; there was much hand-wringing by ministers, politicians, and teachers about the misbehavior of younger people, disrespect for authority, and so forth. A fairly complete inventory and discussion of the alleged US failures was pulled together in Harold Stearns's *Civilization in the United States: An Inquiry by Thirty Americans* (1922), which argued that the country was in a state of "emotional and aesthetic starvation," that it possessed "no heritages or traditions to which to cling except those that have already withered in our hands and turned to dust," and that it was in need of total change if it was to overcome its "spiritual poverty."

There were frequent assaults by writers on the culture of prosperity, purity, and political normalcy. Sinclair Lewis's *Babbitt* (1922) was a major novel that satirized the upper-class culture of a small Midwestern city, including its antiunion, antiradical, antiethnic, and anti-Semitic attitudes as well as the main character's pathetic and unsuccessful efforts to break away into an extramarital affair and an involvement in the local bohemia. William Carlos Williams's "To Elsie," one of the poems in his *Spring and All* (1922), began with the lines "The pure products of America / go crazy" and went on to lyrically portray the sorts of disabilities that were produced when a culture became isolated and inbred across generations. Williams's subject was the so-called "Jackson Whites" of the north Jersey mountains, a small group, widely discussed in the popular press, which had lived isolated from outsiders since the late eighteenth century, but he was no doubt speaking metaphorically. F. Scott Fitzgerald's "May Day," a 1920 story, is an ironic, sardonic account of the irrational, gratuitous, antiradical violence of the summer of 1919. May Day, the first day of May, was traditionally when springtime renewal was celebrated; in the modern world, May 1 had already become in nearly all countries a day for honoring labor (the US did not participate). May Day in Fitzgerald's story is a day of random mob violence, rioting, and a great deal of drinking in which the stupidity and misbehavior of wealthy college students duplicates the misbehavior and stupidity of ordinary folk.

The expansion of college education in the 1920s was celebrated in the mainstream press as a sign of prosperity and progress. Writers, on the other hand, usually saw college students as pampered dumbbells or mediocrities and colleges as places that did not produce knowledge or authentic character. This view, the same as the one in Jack London's "South of the Slot," runs through "May Day" and is only slightly softened in Fitzgerald's 1920 Princeton novel, *This Side of Paradise*. It is laid out at length in Upton Sinclair's nonfiction *The Goose-Step: A Study of American Higher Education* (1923), his encyclopedic and sometimes hilarious documentary account of the corporate control of colleges and the shallow educations that those colleges typically perpetrated on their unthinking conformist students. Fitzgerald's *The Great Gatsby* (1925) includes an implicit critique of college education, while Cather's *The Professor's House* (1925) contains a very explicit critique.

The Great Gatsby, probably the most read American novel written in the 1920s, reflects and articulates many of the mainstream culture's central themes and concerns. It asserts the role of "good breeding" in the formation of character and its narrator expresses conventional prejudices about blacks, Jews, and others. It explores conventional ideas about the sources of wealth, how wealth ought to be displayed, and the morality (and criminality) of its wealthy central characters. Set in 1922, shortly after the beginning of Prohibition, its characters nonetheless drink a great deal and its main character, Jay Gatsby, is a major player in the illegal alcohol trade. At its conclusion, it argues that the "Westerners" in the novel should never have moved to the corrupt east coast but should have stayed out where the "dark fields of the republic" existed, that is, in the "real" America.

The Great Gatsby is narrated, and therefore shaped, by Nick Carraway, who in his first few paragraphs provides readers with core information about his outlook. Much of that information indicates his sense of himself as superior and privileged. First of all, he tells us, he is "inclined to reserve all judgments," a quality that has often led people to open themselves up to him. Second, he says he was taught by his father that "a sense of the fundamental decencies is parceled out unequally at birth." Third, he says that the events he describes in the book taught him that his tolerance has limits and that Gatsby, who he says "represented everything for which I have an unaffected scorn," had "turned out all right at the end" (an odd statement because at the end Gatsby was dead). Fourth, he tells us that he is well-bred, coming from a wealthy Midwestern family, that he graduated from Yale in 1915, that he served during the war, and that, financed by his father, he moved east in 1922 in order to learn the bond business (later, though, he says that he also came east to avoid getting married). Nick lives in a bungalow in a Long Island suburb of New York City and has "a dog … and an old Dodge and a Finnish woman, who made my bed and cooked breakfast and muttered Finnish wisdom to herself over the electric stove." His paralleling of an ethnic housekeeper with an animal and an automobile indicates, obviously, a severe kind of condescension.

In Chapter 4 of *Gatsby*, there are more condescending comments by Nick about other "non-Americans." Driving into Manhattan, he observes a group of people "with the tragic eyes and short upper lips of southeastern Europe," a stock image of Italians. A few lines later, in a "role reversal" scene containing standard racist language, the car he is in is passed by a limousine "driven by a white chauffeur, in which sat three modish negroes, two bucks and a girl. I laughed aloud as the yolks of their eyeballs rolled toward us in haughty rivalry." At lunch that same day, he is introduced by Gatsby to Meyer Wolfsheim, who Nick initially describes, in the conventional language of anti-Semitism, as a "small, flat-nosed Jew" who "raised his large head and regarded me with two fine growths of hair which luxuriated in either nostril," who looks out at the world through "tiny" eyes, who speaks of a business "gonnection" and "Oggsford" College, who eats with "ferocious delicacy," and who wears cufflinks made of human molars. Later, Wolfsheim is said to have been the man who fixed the 1919 World Series. Near the end of the book, we learn that Wolfsheim believes that he raised Gatsby "right out of the gutter," that he suggested that Gatsby join the American Legion, and that Gatsby first worked for an Albany, NY, client of Wolfsheim. The comment about the American Legion indicates Wolfsheim's understanding of the importance of appearing patriotic, while the comment about the client in Albany indicates that one part of his business is political (Albany is the capital of New York State that was widely reputed to be full of corrupt politicians and lobbyists).

Nick has conventional attitudes about race and ethnicity. His very rich Yale classmate, Tom Buchanan, has white supremacist beliefs. When we first meet him, Tom talks about his reading of Theodore Lothrop Stoddard's popular *The Rising Tide of Color Against White World-Supremacy* (1920), one of a number of contemporary books which argued that white supremacy was threatened. Tom gets the title and author's name slightly wrong, which suggests he has not been reading it very closely, but summarizes what he takes to be the key points: that "if we don't look out the white race will be – will be utterly submerged" and that "It's up to us, who are the dominant race, to watch out or these other races will have control of things." Tom is presented as supercilious, muscular, brutal, blunt, dumb, inarticulate, offensive, and hulking; in college he played football, now he plays polo. Oddly enough for a man who believes so deeply in social hierarchy, Tom has an affair with the working-class Myrtle Wilson, whose efforts to take on upper-class airs are harshly satirized by Nick.

The Great Gatsby is a novel of wealth in the tradition of Henry James and Edith Wharton. It involves two different kinds of wealthy people, those who inherited their money and those who got it through their own work; at the beginning of Chapter 4 the long lists of East Egg and West Egg residents, the former having Anglo surnames and the latter including a number of people with Irish and Jewish surnames, efficiently lay out the general distinction. Tom and Daisy Buchanan have inherited their wealth, as has Nick Carraway. Jay Gatsby has made his own money, he is a self-made man. But Gatsby's story is not the traditional one about the hard-working, determined, inventive man who rises and does good things for others. Rather, as told by Nick, Gatsby is a child of the hardscrabble West who seized the opportunities resulting from his wartime service, anglicized his name from Gatz to Gatsby, took on pseudo-British ways and bits of language like "old sport," and is the partner of Meyer Wolfsheim, the Jew who corrupted baseball (the "game of democracy," as it was often called), in criminal enterprises that include bootlegging and trading in stolen bonds. This is definitely *not* the stuff of the "American dream," the short-hand descriptive phrase that began to be used in the 1930s, during the Great Depression, and that has sometimes been read back into *The Great Gatsby*.

The core difference between old money and ill-gotten new money is symbolized by the mansions occupied by the Buchanans and Gatsby and by Gatsby's car. The Buchanan mansion is described as an elaborate Georgian Colonial with a quarter mile of lawn and gardens separating it from the beach. The view from the front included "in its sweep a sunken Italian garden, a half acre of deep, pungent roses, and a snub-nosed motorboat that bumped the tide offshore." Its interior, when first seen by Nick, is a "bright rosy-colored space" full of whiteness and gentle breezes that lifted curtains toward the "frosted wedding-cake of the ceiling, and then rippled over the wine-colored rug, making a shadow on it as wind does on the sea." It is the sort of overdone Colonial Revival house often pictured in contemporary magazines like *Country Life* as suitable dwellings for "rooted," wealthy, 100 percent Americans. In contrast, Gatsby's mansion is "a factual imitation of some Hotel de Ville in Normandy, with a tower on one side, spanking new under a thick beard of raw ivy, and a marble swimming pool, and more than forty acres of lawn and garden." It is a foreign fraud imposed on the landscape or, as Nick says at the end of the novel, "a huge incoherent failure of a house." Gatsby's "gorgeous" car deepens the point about his overdone incoherence: it is "a rich cream color, bright with nickel, swollen here and there in its monstrous length with triumphant hat-boxes and supper-boxes, and terraced with a labyrinth of wind-shields that mirrored a dozen suns." The words "swollen," "monstrous," and "labyrinth" emphasize the obese disharmonies of its design, while the "dozen suns" suggest the distortions of carnival funhouse mirrors and raise the question of whether anything could be accurately seen through those windshields.

When it became time for him to assess the characters in *Gatsby* in terms of their decency, honesty, and humanity, Nick Carraway was not presented with ambiguities. The partygoers are dismissed as only interested in enjoying themselves. Wolfsheim is a criminal who says that he realized when he first met Gatsby that he "could use him good." Jordan Baker is "incurably dishonest." Daisy is superficial, dishonest, materialistic, and the perpetrator of a hit-and-run vehicular homicide that she allows Gatsby to take the blame for and be killed for in a murder enabled by her husband. Tom, in addition to all of his other negative qualities, is an accessory to murder. Together, in Nick's very strange, understated indictment, the Buchanans were "careless people" who "smashed up things and creatures and then retreated back into their money or their vast carelessness, or whatever it was that kept them together, and let other people clean up the mess they had made."

Gatsby, while a fake and a criminal, is judged by Nick as better than all the others. At the beginning of the novel, in the passage in which Nick says that Gatsby represented "everything for which I have an unaffected scorn," he also says that there was "something gorgeous about him" and that he had "an extraordinary gift for hope." Later, with bemused admiration, he says that Gatsby's dream of possessing Daisy had led him into the "colossal vitality of his illusion" that became a "creative passion" for her. He is clearly better than the other characters. I am not sure that that says a lot, however.

In a huge jump from the particular to the general, Nick Carraway concludes that the story he tells in the novel is about how Westerners like himself, Gatsby, the Buchanans, and Jordan Baker "possessed some deficiency in common which made us subtly unadaptable to Eastern life." This statement comes in the closing pages of the novel, just after Nick recalls his youth in what he describes as a winter wonderland of "street lamps and sleigh bells in the frosty dark and the shadows of holly wreaths thrown by lighted windows on the snow" and life in a city in which houses are still called by a family's name (as in "The Carraway House"). It comes just before he describes the East as a place of "distortion" that has given him "fantastic dreams" of surreal events. Warm memories of picture-book Midwest winter scenes and the social stability symbolized by the persistence of old houses known by family names, along with his general revulsion about the East, lead him to announce that he "decided to come back home" (that sentence with its "come back home" instead of "go back home" indicates, I think, that Nick was telling his story to a sympathetic Midwesterner).

In short, a three-month experience of life among the wealthy in the New York suburbs was enough to convince Nick of where, so to speak, his real America existed. The last few paragraphs of *Gatsby* reiterate this conclusion at a more abstract level: in them, we are taken back to the "green breast of the new world," then to Gatsby's experience and then to Nick's statement that Gatsby's mistake was that he did not know that his dream was in reality "somewhere back in that vast obscurity beyond the city, where the dark fields of the republic rolled on under the night."

Another classic fiction, Willa Cather's *The Professor's House*, published a few months after *The Great Gatsby* in 1925, is also engaged with themes about how wealth is used, what houses express about their residents, and where the authentic America exists. The novel explores conflicting points of view about the good life, contrasting Professor Godfrey St. Peter's tradition-bound interests with the materialistic interests of his wife and family. Set in a small Midwestern college town, it explores the world of the dumbed-down, commercialized university. Ultimately, it explores the memories and desires of the Professor who believes that "His career, his wife, his family, were not his life at all, but a chain of events which had happened to him" and who is seeking replenishment in the time he has left.

As in *Gatsby*, there are contrasting houses in *The Professor's House* that are used symbolically: the professor's old, unfashionable house in which he insists on staying; the new fashionable house he and his wife recently purchased with the $20,000 prize he received for his award-winning eight-volume study of the Spanish explorers of North America; the "Norwegian manor house" one of his daughters and her husband (a materialistic Jew who is able to pass as a Gentile because "There was nothing Semitic about his countenance except his nose") is building on the shoreline of Lake Michigan with the money the daughter inherited from Tom Outland, the Professor's best and brightest student; the "bungalow" of the less wealthy daughter and son-in-law; the pre-Columbian pueblo dwellings located on Mesa Verde in the southwestern corner of Colorado.

The cliff dwellings of Mesa Verde were built by the Anasazi people around AD 500, abandoned by them around AD 1200, "discovered" by local ranchers in 1888, and preserved as the centerpiece of Mesa Verde National Park when it was created in 1906. Cather narrates a version of that discovery in the section of *The Professor's House* titled "Tom Outland's Story" when Tom rides into the wild mesa, looks up at a cliff, and sees there a "a little city of stone, asleep." Tom describes his initial impressions of the "pale little houses of stone nestling close to one another, perched on top of each other, with flat roofs, narrow windows, straight walls, and in the middle of the group, a round tower." He then comments on the beauty of the tower, the "immortal repose" of the scene, the "calmness of eternity" that it conveyed, and its "special kind of solemnity." Later on in "Tom Outland's Story," a local Catholic priest who worked among contemporary Native Americans remarks on the old culture's artfulness and general superiority, says it must have been very complex "compared to that of our roving Navajos," and speculates that it was wiped out by "some roving Indian tribe without culture or domestic virtues." Contained in those remarks, as I read them, is considerable hostility to the Native Americans who now inhabit the area and perhaps a theory about the decline and degeneration of Native American culture before the arrival of Europeans. The priest's notion of the good Indians being wiped out by bad Indians has in no way been authenticated by later archaeological work at Mesa Verde of other Anasazi sites.

The lost Anasazi culture functions in *The Professor's House* as the spiritual and aesthetic alternative to the materialism and emptiness of the twentieth century. Obviously, Professor St. Peter cannot travel back into it as Nick Carraway returns to his stable and picturesque Midwest. But near the end of the novel he decides that next summer he will go "down into Outland's country, to watch the sunrise break on sculptured peaks and impassable mountain passes – to look off at those long, rugged, untamed vistas dear to the American heart." Later on, just after he speaks of the "chain of events" that formed his life, he says that he has rediscovered himself as the Kansas boy he once was: "He was a primitive. He was only interested in earth and woods and water." This epiphany leads him to Zen-like (or perhaps Anasazi-like) recognitions such as "He was earth, and would return to earth. When white clouds blew over the lake like bellying sails, when the seven pine-trees turned red in the declining sun, he felt satisfaction and said to himself merely: 'That is right.'" The sort of natural religion rhetoric employed by Cather to describe the Professor's feelings parallels the rhetoric used by people involved in the various late nineteen- and early twentieth-century movements to create national parks to pre-serve wildness and to give overcivilized, urbanized Americans places in what was often called "nature's cathedrals" to meditate and replenish themselves. Cather's comments about what was to be learned from the Anasazi people are unique, however, because Mesa Verde was the only national park created to protect and preserve an environment constructed by human beings.

"Primitivism" is the belief that life was better or more moral during the early stages of humankind or among primitive people and has deteriorated with civilization. In the early twentieth century, and especially in the 1920s, there was a great interest in "primitive" art, the indigenous arts of Africa, Oceania, and North America (such as those of the Anasazi and other southwest Native Americans). These definitions, I think, help to connect *The Professor's House* to a particular intellectual milieu. They may help to clarify Nick Carraway's retreat to his simpler Midwest. They also apply to and help us to understand a number of other classic 1920s literary works. Katherine Anne Porter's first story, the 1922 "Maria Concepcion," exalts the self-reliant serenity and toughness of its 18-year-old heroine who walks with "the free, natural, guarded ease of the primitive woman carrying an unborn child" and who, after she murders her husband's mistress, is last seen "resting deliciously" while holding the murdered woman's newborn baby. Sherwood Anderson's *Dark Laughter* (1925), the most popular book he ever wrote, contrasted empty, meaningless, "modern" lives with the allegedly happy, carefree, natural lives of black people. Some of Ernest Hemingway's Nick Adams stories implicitly contrasted the character's wartime experiences with his experiences in the far reaches of Michigan's remote Upper Peninsula. "Big Two-Hearted River" narrates Nick's solitary replenishment on a fishing trip, involves his going backward from civilization and, just as important, his use of very old-fashioned camping and fishing techniques (trout fishing in the 1920s was becoming a rich man's sport involving lots of expensive paraphernalia, strictures against using live bait, and so forth). Hemingway's *The Sun Also Rises* (1926) involves many scenes watching and parsing "primitive" bullfights, fishing scenes in the pure waters of the Spanish Pyrenees, scenes with soulful peasants, and, as an obvious contrast to the Prohibition era, much joyful drinking of simple wine. The novel also includes a college-educated Jew, Robert Cohn, who is not a member of the in-group.

A sharp and funny satire on the idea of renewal through nature is contained in Chapter 11 of Lewis's *Babbitt*, in which Babbitt goes with a friend to a Maine fishing resort and is "converted to serenity." Hemingway's *The Torrents of Spring* (1926) satirizes Sherwood Anderson's *Dark Laughter*, substituting Native American characters for Anderson's wise and natural black characters.

Politicians and others in the postwar years tried to create a pure, prosperous, and normal America that was just like the America they imagined had actually existed in times past. Many writers responded with work that challenged these impulses but that sometimes also sought purity, stability, and authenticity (instead of prosperity) in imagined pasts.

Black writers of the 1920s, the writers of the Harlem Renaissance, produced a number of lasting works and some classics such as Langston Hughes's poems "The Negro Speaks of Rivers" and "The Weary Blues," books like Jean Toomer's brilliant Modernist *Cane* (1923) and Nella Larsen's *Passing* (1929), and stories like Zora Neale Hurston's "Sweat" and "The Eatonville Anthology." Little of this distinguished writing engaged the public policy issues of the day, only small parts of it could be called "social protest" writing, none of it took part in the grand debates about the national past and destiny, and none of it, so far as I am aware, was involved with "primitivism." Instead, black writing of the 1920s attempted to represent how black Americans actually lived in their communities, how black institutions in those communities functioned, how people related to each other, how they spoke, what they did with their time, and so forth. Toomer's work and Hurston's were especially penetrating about the lives of southern blacks. Larsen's novel was especially acute regarding skin color as a determinant of social class within the black community. Hughes's poems, as well as poems by writers such as Claude McKay, Countee Cullen, and Gwendolyn B. Bennett, often presented black American desires and social aspirations.

In some ways, black writers of the 1920s anticipated the work of both black and white writers of the Great Depression, when the social contexts of American writing shifted dramatically and when the question of who ordinary people, black and white, actually were and how they lived became far more pressing than it had been in earlier years.

Index

*Index compiled by Meg Davies (Fellow
of the Society of Indexers)*